Millennials in Wonderland

Millennials in Wonderland

Coaching Grads at the Crossroads of Life and Career

Wendy Schuman and Kenneth Schuman

ISBN-13: 9780692885222
ISBN-10: 0692885226

DEDICATION

*To the coaches, who empower young people to find their path
and fulfill their dreams.*

To the graduates, whose courage and optimism give us hope for the future.

*To Andy and Cory, our own Millennial and Gen Xer, who taught
us to listen.*

TABLE OF CONTENTS

INTRODUCTION

By Wendy Schuman

> *"Tell me, what is it you plan to do with*
> *your one wild and precious life?"*
> —MARY OLIVER

The story of *Alice in Wonderland* holds a powerful analogy for today's college grads: Alice is lost in a forest of confusing pathways and conflicting directions. Seeing a Cheshire cat in a tree, she asks, "Which road do I take?" (She must be desperate, because cats are notably uncommunicative.) "Where do you want to go?" is his response. "I don't know," says the distraught Alice. "Then," says the cat, fading away, "it doesn't matter."

But finding the path to a life of meaning and fulfillment does indeed matter. Yes, the world is full of wonders, but many young people are left wondering about their future. Thousands of them pour out of colleges annually as confused as Alice, asking, "What should I do with my life?" And even if they think they've got it figured out, our society isn't exactly waiting for them with open arms.

What is the world like today for recent college grads? Vastly different from the one young people faced even a few years ago. Old industries are disappearing while new ones—fueled by technology, big data, analytics, and connectivity—are taking shape. Economic disruptions have become the norm. Many jobs have moved overseas, and full-time, permanent employment for those without experience has become rare. Even though job creation has been increasing, the trend is skewed by a rise in part-time jobs. Plus, the growth of the "gig economy" means that many grads can expect to begin a new job search every few months or even weeks.

Imagine trying to gain a foothold in this slippery terrain while simultaneously making the biggest developmental transition of your life—becoming a full-fledged, independent adult, leaving the structured (and sheltered) environment of college, and entering a world of almost constant rejection. Most grads describe applying to jobs online and sending hundreds of résumés into a black cyber-hole from which they get no response. Even when some have managed to get an interview, they often hear nothing back. Many fall down this rabbit hole and never recover their footing. This is a troubling issue, and it's not an abstract one. Indeed, it affects everyone who cares about the future of young people and the nation.

Think of the numbers involved: Millennials (those born between approximately 1982 and 2004) have surpassed Baby Boomers as the nation's largest living generation, according to population estimates released in April 2016 by the U.S. Census Bureau. They now number 75.4 million. That's a huge cohort of educated young people out there looking for jobs, which haven't been quick in coming. A Rutgers University study found that "half the college graduates from 2010 were still job searching a year later." The 2017 U.S. Census Bureau report estimates that a third of 18- to 34-year-olds in the U.S. live at home. Among the 25- to 34-year-olds living at home, one in four is neither enrolled in school nor working. Research by Yale economist Lisa B. Kahn shows that those who can't get a job in the first few years after graduation fall permanently behind in terms of salary—and perhaps life satisfaction. We can't afford to leave a generation unproductive, dazed, and confused.

The Good, or Actually Amazing, News About Coaching

At the crossroads where college intersects with "real life," coaches can make a crucial difference for young adults. At a pivotal moment, coaching can help the emerging generation make both a living and a life. As coach Valerie Dorn explains in Chapter 1 ("Finding a Job: The 7 Biggest Challenges for Millennials"), "Millennials are still figuring out who they are, what they value, and what success means to them. As a coach, you have an incredible opportunity to support and guide them so that they can create a successful, *repeatable* process for finding the first job—or the next job—that is the right fit for them. You have an opportunity to support young grads as they navigate the potentially stormy waters between graduation and establishing themselves in an initial career path...to educate and empower clients to create their own unique path forward toward their dreams and goals."

Helping young people to create more wonder and less wondering. That's what this book is about.

It Started with a Pro Bono Coaching Program

First, a little background. In 2012, my husband Ken and I started Grad Life Choices, a volunteer coaching program, to bring experienced life and career coaches to the aid of Millennials who were caught short after the Great Recession of 2008. We witnessed firsthand and in news reports that young people were graduating from college burdened by heavy debt in the midst of a serious economic downturn. An AP analysis of government data for 2012 determined that "half of young college graduates [are] either jobless or underemployed in positions that don't fully use their skills and knowledge." We feared that widespread joblessness was leaving deep scars that could remain long after the economy picked up. Millennials were in danger of becoming a lost generation.

The bottom line: Grads were losing the sense of fairness of the American system. They had been promised that if they played by the rules—studied hard, finished school, developed skills, and invested in their education—their futures would be bright. But this wasn't happening. They were confronting their future with extensive unemployment and no plan as to how to deal with it. When we started our program, many of the young people who contacted us were discouraged or depressed, their confidence shattered. Some described themselves as "paralyzed."

One of the grads who reached out had been fruitlessly searching for a full-time job for three years post-graduation. He wrote, "The countless no's, no responses, and things ultimately not working out have beaten my spirit to the point where enough is enough. Getting my hopes up, having belief and faith that it will work out, doing the work—and for it to still not work out—has taken its toll. I feel like giving up."

Many emails were heart-breaking. One young woman wrote: "I have no one to help me and I've been on my own since I was 17. I was a wonderful student and graduated from college in Georgia with a 3.79 GPA. I have no idea how I have dropped the ball so badly since I graduated and I'm starting to lose hope. I seem to have no ability to find a decent job. I worked way too hard in school to end up waiting tables."

We realized that this generation could benefit enormously from coaching, but few young people could afford the cost. Many were either unemployed or underemployed, working in low-wage or part-time jobs, or working in unpaid internships. They were up to their ears in college debt. Many parents, who had spent or borrowed thousands of dollars to pay for their children's education, in many cases sacrificing their own retirement savings, were tapped out.

So we set up Grad Life Choices to match unemployed or underemployed graduates with experienced life and career coaches who would be willing to take on one young person each on a pro bono basis. Each grad would receive 12 free hours of coaching, usually over the course of three months—enough, we hoped, to get them out of paralysis mode, develop a plan, and jump-start their careers.

We put out a call for help to all the coaches we knew and to many others through coach newsletters and groups. Coaches are famously generous and public-spirited people. The response of the coaching community was phenomenal. Over the last five years more than 85 life and career coaches around the country (including Alaska), all professionally trained through recognized coaching programs and certified by the International Coach Federation, volunteered to work with these young adults one-on-one by phone or Skype.

The coaches have been nothing short of inspirational. Their deep coaching skills, along with personal qualities of generosity, empathy, and positivity, enabled them over the last four years to help more than 230 grads move ahead with their lives and careers. Many coaches re-upped multiple times, helping numerous grads free of charge. Some have continued to work with their young clients past the allotted 12 sessions, vowing to stick with them until they found a job.

What's in it for coaches? Some of them explained:

"I remember how alone and lost I felt graduating from college even in a booming job market! So I feel passionately about helping recent grads get a solid foundation under them – particularly to help give them a sense of expanded possibility and sense of strength of self for what they can create for their lives." —Melissa Maher

"I did not have an opportunity like this and I know it is important to share and give back. Initially, I thought of it as an opportunity to build my coaching skills and hours. Now, it is much more than this." —Vanessa Blacknall-Jamison

"I remember what it was like to be a recent grad looking to start my career. Lots of obstacles that years later I realized weren't as big as they seemed at the time. I liked the idea of helping recent grads build their self-awareness and develop their emotional intelligence to recognize obstacles for what they are and not to make them out to be bigger than they are." —Cindy Weingartner

"I am very interested in helping young people discover their gifts and purpose in life and helping them design a plan to achieve their goals as well as make a contribution to something greater than themselves. I saw this as an opportunity to give back and accomplish more of my purpose—win/win." —Leigh Higgins

Coaching Millennials: How It's Different

One thing we observed early on was that coaching young people in their 20s is different from coaching other generations. Gen Xers and Baby Boomers have years of experience in life and work. They come to coaching with the desire to reboot their lives or change their careers. By contrast, Millennials, or Gen Y, are on the brink of starting their adult lives and professions, so their experience and practical knowledge are necessarily limited. Coaches in the program were delighted to have a chance to assist this important rising demographic. The challenge, though, was working with an age group that few had coached before.

When we looked for resources to help coaches work with Millennials—and to help the grads themselves get the most out of coaching—we found scattered print and online articles, but no single book that pulled all the information together.

Millennials in Wonderland exists to fill that information gap. We realized that over the last few years, the coaches volunteering for Grad Life Choices probably had more experience coaching Millennials than anyone in the field. They themselves were the experts. So when we asked nearly two dozen of them to contribute chapters to this book, they were excited to share the knowledge they've gained on all different aspects of coaching this smart, creative, diverse, and challenging generation.

What we learned from the coaches was this: No matter how insurmountable the problems, there are solutions that work. In this book, the coaches take on the full range of Millennial concerns, including:

- How to choose a career even if you have no idea what to do (and your major seems totally useless).
- How to create a sustaining "life vision," using strengths, values, and passions to determine your future.
- Coping with discouragement and inertia, and developing grit and motivation to overcome setbacks.
- Setting goals and action steps for a career plan—and staying on course.
- Using career and personality assessments.
- Creating great résumés and stand-out cover letters that get through computerized applicant tracking systems.
- Getting and nailing interviews.
- Developing critical networking skills.
- Tapping into the benefits of social media for job search.
- When to seek out advanced education—and when not to.

- Overcoming blocks and negativity to build self-confidence.
- Dealing with crushing education debt.
- Issues around moving back home with parents.
- Coaching grads who have mental health issues.

These issues and many others in the book are tackled by the coaches with compassion, intelligence, and skill. Through vivid case histories and step-by-step approaches, the coaches demonstrate how they have adapted tried-and-true coaching techniques and exercises to the special characteristics and needs of young adult clients. There are 24 coach-written chapters filled with practical tips, how-to's, and wisdom. You can dip into a particular chapter to learn about a specific issue or read the book straight through.

You'll read what works and what doesn't. As Valerie Dorn notes, "In working with Millennials, I have found that they are looking for someone to tell them what to do. They want 'the answer'—a clearly defined path from where they are now to where they think they want to go. As a coach, you can help graduates become more comfortable with uncertainty and more confident in themselves and their choices."

But there are times when coaches find it best to diverge from "pure" coaching and to broaden their role. As coach Leigh Higgins writes, "In the traditional coaching model, coaches are not mentors. We are empowerment and transition specialists. However, young clients generally do not have the extensive networking contacts or work experience to develop a frame of reference for what they want to do. Or they don't necessarily know the reality of what that work looks like in practice." So coaches may sometimes need to put on their mentoring or consulting hat to help their young clients' unlock their potential.

Success Stories

We were greatly inspired by the determination and drive of young people in the program, many of whom who overcame even the most dire circumstances to find jobs in their career field. With their coaches' help, they achieved breakthroughs, sometimes after years of unemployment and rejection. Here are some of their stories, and you'll find others throughout the book. (Note: The names of the graduates in this book have been changed to preserve their privacy.)

- Lawrence was a communications major from a poor family in the South Bronx. For three years after graduating from an elite college (he was on scholarship), he was unable to find fulltime work. He kept taking temporary writing and marketing gigs that never turned into anything permanent. At one point, he was almost homeless and considered joining the military to find stability. With the unwavering support of his coach, he finally was hired as a fulltime social media producer for a major cable channel.

- Maya, who had a B.A. and a master's in public health (with $90,000 in college loans), was working part-time at a Rite Aid. With coaching help, she found a position as a science teacher in a NYC charter school.

- James lost his father in the 9/11 attacks when he was 8 years old. A graduate of a state university, he was working as a valet at a golf course. Coaching gave him the confidence to pursue his dream of working in sports management, where he coordinates partnerships for professional competitions.

- Eleanor had a degree in international relations and was in a program to become a physical therapist. However, she dropped out when she realized she lacked the commitment of the other students. In addition, she had been hospitalized for an eating disorder and was living in a halfway house after treatment. Working with a coach, she discovered a passion for nonprofit work and became office manager for an organization that helps at-risk youth.

- Gina was a paralegal who hated her job, but she was so stressed at work that she didn't have time to explore a different career. Coaching helped her find her passion and create a plan to make time for her job search. The result: She found a job in the policy department of Meetup, a large network of local interest groups.

These and many other real-life examples of challenges and successes in the book are profoundly reassuring. Confusion after college is not only extremely common, it can also be a source of strength. As coach Deborah Tyson explains in Chapter 6 ("But What Can I Do with My Life?"): "I see early career turmoil as a rite of passage and something that is required to give them the motivation to look for something different and more in line with who they are. My experience has told me, and my deep belief in the coaching modality has shown me, that we always know deep down what is best for us. We just often need help uncovering it."

This Book Is Not Only for Coaches

We've created this book to be used not just by coaches, but by Millennials themselves and by those who care about or work with them—parents, college counselors, mentors, career development professionals, employers, and managers of this generation. You'll learn how to help young adults move forward toward economic independence and personal growth—and inspire them to unlock their potential. Grads will also gain a better understanding of how coaching works and thus be able to benefit more quickly. Many of the chapters can be immediately applied to their own situations. As one grad, Molly, recalls: "I initially sought coaching because I was at a crossroads. I was eager to try anything new so long as I was learning, growing, and serving others. Coaching, for me, was about identifying and integrating my core values. Over the course of three months, I became more and more invigorated by the fact that I feel 100% in control of the conditions of my life, and that a good deal of that control comes from my ability to employ and have faith in my values."

Millennials: They're Different than You Might Think

We've conducted our own research based on surveys of Millennials and their coaches in our program, and our findings are laid out in our final chapter. Together, they form a picture of this generation's greatest needs, concerns, and assets. Unlike the prevailing stereotype of Millennials as narcissistic, entitled whiners, coddled by their parents and schools, the young people surveyed are neither well-to-do nor entitled. Most come from middle-class or low-income families, reflecting the U.S. population as a whole. Many are first-generation college grads, some even the first in their family to graduate from high school. The huge debt so many grads have incurred makes it impossible for them to take unpaid internships. They don't sit around crying—they take menial jobs to make ends meet while trying to reach for a better life. But they find themselves in a tough spot: entering a very challenging economy without contacts or support necessary to gain access to decent jobs. (See Chapter 17, "First in the Family: Coaching First-Generation College Grads.") So one of the goals of coaching is to level the playing field, providing the kind of support and resources that are common in more privileged families. It is our hope that these findings will contribute to the body of knowledge on what helps Millennials thrive and how coaches can assist them.

Most importantly, Millennials are not treated as cartoonish figures, but as young adults deserving of compassion and respect. They're idealistic—they want to change the world, and as the first generation of digital natives, they have the tools to do it. As Deborah Tyson notes, "Millennials are part of a generation that is shaking up the status quo. The options are truly endless, which is often part of the trouble. Partnering with a trusted coach, advisor, or mentor who can help them explore their true interests and strengths, free of judgment, is often just what it takes for a recent grad to figure out this puzzle. It's amazing what the coach and grad uncover together. The answers truly are waiting for them. This answer won't come from a book, a blog, a video, or a person; it can only come from them."

Millennials are already the largest generation in the workplace, with more arriving every day. Our future depends on helping them flourish and be the best they can be.

We are profoundly grateful to the coaches who contributed chapters to this book—and to all the coaches who participate in the important mission of helping young people face the future with a plan and a sense of hope, leading them to create independent lives of purpose and fulfillment.

PART I: GETTING UNSTUCK

CHAPTER 1

FINDING A JOB: THE 7 BIGGEST CHALLENGES FOR MILLENNIALS

By Valerie Dorn

> *"I never expected to be in this underemployment poverty situation and certainly not for as long as it's lasted. My sense of self has definitely taken a hit. This has taken a toll in interviews and in my general application approach. I am no longer certain what I can do with my degree or what I want to do."*
> —OLIVIA

As a coach, you have an incredible opportunity to support recent college graduates as they navigate the potentially stormy waters between graduation and establishing themselves in an initial career path. In coaching recent college grads, the most important thing to understand is their developmental level. They have recently moved from adolescence into young adulthood; from a structured environment with lots of external reinforcement and a clear roadmap to an open and uncertain future without clear directions. Millennials are simultaneously excited and overwhelmed by the possibilities before them. But they can become discouraged when they do not land their dream job immediately upon graduating from college or graduate school.

Each of the challenges described below is an opportunity to educate and empower clients to create their own unique path forward toward their dreams and goals.

Challenge #1: Holding on to beliefs that no longer serve them.

I worked with a client in her 20s who had studied engineering in college and started a career in engineering. After a few years she was laid off and had been unemployed for almost a year when we started working together. She did not have any energy or enthusiasm for her job search, which, as it turned out, was because she no longer wanted to be an engineer. After giving herself permission to think beyond what she had gone to school for, she discovered that she actually had a passion for teaching girls math and science. After volunteering at a public school for a couple of months, she realized that teaching was a perfect fit for her. All she needed to pursue this new path was to obtain teaching certification, and there were several accelerated programs that would enable her to begin her new teaching career in only a year.

As a coach, you can help young adult clients expand their idea of what they think is possible and encourage them to be open to new possibilities. Often twentysomethings think it is too late for them to change direction, or believe that if they do something different, then everything that they have done up until now has been a waste. Help them to see that their past experience and education is not only valuable but also a necessary step along the way to where they are going. Also, coach them around fears and false expectations. Their first (or second or third) job will not be their last and only job; it is OK to use the next job as a stepping stone to bring them closer to their ideal job. Help clients to see the bigger picture—young college grads are not used to thinking beyond a semester or a year at a time, so they often have anxiety about how long they think they will "have" to be in their next job.

Guiding Questions:

- How do you define success?
- What is your inner voice telling you?
- When you think of the future, what are you afraid of?

Challenge #2: Not recognizing their own strengths and values.

In working with Millennials, I have found that many of them do not recognize or know how to articulate what their skills are and how that translates into a job. For example, I worked with a recent college graduate, Sherry, who did not think she was qualified for the jobs she wanted to apply for. Together we broke down the job descriptions into concrete skills and compared them to her experiences on her resume. Sherry had extensive experience working in retail, which she thought was menial and irrelevant. However, upon closer examination she realized that she had supervised and trained new associates, which demonstrated leadership skills that she thought she was lacking. We went through her resume one experience at a time, including work, volunteer, and extracurricular activities. By the end of our conversation, Sherry was not only clear about what she had to offer an employer, but was also feeling confident in applying for the positions she wanted, understanding her value for the first time.

Another critical aspect to a successful job search is having a clear understanding of one's values and how they connect to finding meaningful work. As a coach, you can help Millennials identify and prioritize their values. There are many free values assessment tools available online and many ways to explore values with clients.

For example, you can have clients focus on their personal values, their work values, or both. For clients who prefer a more kinesthetic approach, you can do a values card sorting activity, organizing values according to their importance. (For a thorough Values Identification exercise, see pages 49-50, Chapter 4, "Creating a Life Vision.")

Assessing values can be especially helpful for clients who do not enjoy the work they are currently doing and/or are not sure what kind of work or work environment they would enjoy. For example, I worked with a recent college graduate whose career interests were quite varied. In addition, she ideally wanted to live and work abroad. After exploring what was most important to her, she came up with her top values: adventure, family, independence, passion, and service. As she reviewed her values and compared them with what she was looking for in a career, she realized that although one of her dreams was to live abroad, she would be more fulfilled if she could live close to her family and incorporate travel into her career by helping others study, work, and live abroad.

Once clients know what they value most, it is often much easier to narrow down their career options across different variables, such as geography, industry, and work environment. My client Angela was living at home with her parents in Pittsburgh and feeling guilty about relying on them. She identified creativity as her highest value but couldn't figure out how to find a job that paid enough for her to live independently and was in a "creative field." She targeted ad agencies and media companies as companies doing creatively interesting work. She was able to find a job as office manager for a media production company and hopes to be able to transition into their filmmaking department.

Guiding Questions:

- What do you value?
- How are your values being honored/not honored at work?

- How important is it to you that certain values are honored at work?
- What are your strengths?
- How closely aligned is your current job with your strengths?
- How important is it to be able to use your strengths at work?

Challenge #3: Not knowing what they want.

Our educational system provides a clear, step-by-step roadmap through college or graduate school, but after that graduates often feel lost, especially if they are not following a more traditionally defined professional career path such as medicine or law. In working with Millennials, I have found that they are looking for someone to tell them what to do. They want "the answer"—a clearly defined path from where they are now to where they think they want to go. For example, I had a client named Leslie who desperately wanted someone to tell her what the correct next step was. She found herself receiving both solicited and unsolicited advice from everyone, and whenever that advice conflicted with her desires, she found herself feeling defensive and resentful.

As a coach, you can help graduates become more comfortable with uncertainty and more confident in themselves and their choices. Through our work together, Leslie decided to stop asking for advice. We came up with strategies for how to respond effectively to unsolicited advice in a way that was respectful to both parties. You can also help clients who do choose to ask for guidance from others to be very specific about what they are looking for, so that the advice they receive is targeted and relevant. As Leslie let go of what others were telling her she should do and started to listen to what she wanted from her heart, her confidence in her own judgment increased. As her self-confidence increased, she was then better able to receive unsolicited advice without it shaking her confidence or direction.

Leslie was also able to stand up for herself in conversations, being more clear with others about what she wanted and why.

Another situation that graduates often find themselves in is being dissatisfied or unhappy in their current job but not knowing what would be better. For example, I worked with Ken, a designer at a graphic design firm. Although he enjoyed his work, he did not like the environment he worked in, which was competitive and critical. It got to the point where he thought he might want to give up graphic design completely—but with further exploration he discovered that maybe it was working specifically in the highly competitive graphic design industry that was contributing to his unhappiness. Ken realized that other industries also needed graphic designers and started applying for in-house design positions in other types of companies. He very quickly landed a position in educational publishing, where he was one of only a few graphic designers in the organization. As a result, his work was deeply appreciated by his non-graphic designer colleagues and he was no longer competing with his co-workers to land good projects.

As a coach, you can help clients home in on the exact elements of their work or work environment that are not a good fit so that they can be clear about what they are looking for in a new job. Help them determine what their top values are (see Challenge #2) and use these to guide their search so that the positions they are applying for are ones in which their top values will be honored. In addition, help clients to develop their self-identity outside of the work that they do. Often graduates equate the type of work that they are doing with their self-worth. Help them find identity and meaning outside of their current position (or lack of employment). For example, they might do volunteering in order to feel that they are helping others and contributing to society. Or they could join a group or take a class in an area they're interested in.

Guiding Questions:

- What do you like most about your current position?
- What do you like least about your current position?
- What would an ideal day look like?
- What skills do you want to gain/develop in your next position?
- What messages have you received from others (family, friends, society) about what kind of work you should be doing?
- What kind of an impact do you want to have through the work that you do?
- How are you taking care of yourself (self-care)?

Challenge #4: Having no clear strategy.

This pitfall results from a combination of Challenges #2 and #3. As a coach, I have seen many graduates applying for jobs using the strategy I call "applying for anything and everything that I think I am qualified for." It is easy for clients to fall into this trap if they lack self-awareness around their strengths and values and don't know what they want. By not being discerning in their search, graduates find themselves feeling overwhelmed, exhausted, frustrated, and fed up with their job search. In addition, they may not be considering positions that are a bit of a stretch for them or may be somewhat outside of their field but might be good stepping stones to build skills to get to their dream job.

For example, I worked with, Lara, a client in her 20s, who after graduation continued to work as a barista at a local coffee shop while applying for any and every position in the country that she thought she might be interested in and qualified for. By the time we started working together, Lara was discouraged by the lack of results and was starting to believe that there was something wrong with her, when in reality the problem was having no clear strategy. Lara said she was willing to relocate anywhere and was applying to a wide variety of positions and industries because her interests were diverse.

As a coach, you can help a client like Lara take time to consider what her top values are and how to use them to narrow her search. Through our work together, Lara was able to limit her geography to a few specific areas of the country and focus on applying for a few different types of positions within one industry: travel. While at first many graduates are worried about narrowing their search too much, with the help of a coach they find that by being more focused, they actually feel more free and successful in their search.

Challenge #5: Feeling isolated.

Looking for a job, especially while living at home, can be very isolating. Graduates go from being surrounded by the support of their peers to being in environments where they may be the only person their age, and thus often feel like no one understands what they are going through. In addition, graduates are used to receiving a lot of external reinforcement in college, and without that, they can feel discouraged and unmotivated. It can be helpful for graduates to seek the support of someone their age who is going through the same process they are, which can be incredibly validating and motivating.

Graduates often compare themselves to their peers, especially through social media, and believe that everyone else has everything figured out—that they have all found jobs they love, are making good salaries, and are living well. As a coach, you can help clients figure out if the time they are spending on social media is supportive or destructive to their confidence and self-esteem. Ask clients how they feel during and after time spent on social media platforms and empower them to limit their time spent on social media if it is having a negative impact on them. Help them find outlets where they can connect with peers in similar situations.

Another challenge many Millennials face is feeling stuck when they are living at home, whether they are currently working or unemployed. It is difficult for them to be motivated to leave the comfort and familiarity of living at home, and they can feel guilty and resentful about being dependent on their parents and family for financial support. On the one hand, they want to be independent and successful living on their own; while on the other hand, there are many benefits and comforts to living at home. Sometimes the safety net of family support can become a crutch. As a coach, you can help graduates living at home identify and weigh the benefits and drawbacks of living at home to help increase their motivation and confidence in finding a job that enables them to move out, if that is their ultimate goal. You can also support them in fostering habits of independence, which can help them feel a sense of autonomy and self-sufficiency. In addition, reassure them with data and anecdotes that they are not alone. All of the major adult milestones are happening later these days—marriage, buying a house, having kids, etc.—so their situation is not uncommon.

Guiding Questions:

- What are your expectations for yourself?
- What do others expect of you?
- How realistic are your expectations and others' expectations?

Challenge #6: 'All or nothing' thinking.

Young adults tend to think in terms of black and white, all or nothing. For example, a client I was working with, Carolyn, told me about how she used her network to land an in-person interview for an ideal position in an organization whose mission was aligned with her goals and vision. In the end, she was not offered the position, and she jumped to the conclusion that "networking does not work." Carolyn truly believed that the entire experience was a failure that she did not want to repeat. I encouraged her to re-examine the situation step-by-step from a different perspective. As we did that together, she realized that although the end result was not what she wanted (the offer of a job), that does not necessarily mean that everything she did along the way was worthless.

As a coach, you can help clients broaden their perspective from viewing situations as being complete successes or failures to include all of the areas in between. Affirm clients' courage in taking steps toward their goal and reinforce their actions that are producing necessary steps on the path to landing a meaningful job. By reinforcing appropriate and effective job search activities, you can help build clients' confidence that the steps they are taking are the "right" steps, even if they do not produce an interview or a job offer every time.

Guiding Question:

- What did you learn from that experience?

Challenge #7: Overreliance on technology and lack of attention to detail.

Millennials are extremely comfortable using technology, and while it can be an incredible tool to use in their job search, it should not be the only tool they are using. I have worked with many clients who had been sending out hundreds of resumes with little to no results. One of the clients I worked with, Cate, had been diligently sending out 10-20 online applications every week and the only response she was receiving was "no" or no response at all. Many Millennials are used to interacting with people online, and it can become too easy to hide behind technology. Cate did not have much experience networking in person and was not sure how to network or where to begin. As a coach, you can help Millennials figure out what their network looks like; most clients are surprised at how big their network actually is and the potential reach of their network. Educate clients on how powerful networking can be and build their confidence that they are able to do it. When Millennials see the value in networking and have confidence in their ability to network, they will not only feel more empowered in their job search but also start to see some concrete results.

Another challenge that I see some Millennials face is a lack of attention to detail in their cover letter and resume. While much of their digital lives do not require perfect spelling or grammar, proofreading cover letters and resumes is absolutely critical for a successful job search. Make sure the clients you are working with have clean, clear, error-free resumes and cover letters. You may need to coach clients around the importance of error-free documents; help them to see the impact that even small mistakes could be having on their success at making it through the initial screening process.

In addition, when working with Millennials, make sure they have sanitized their social media profiles. Many employers screen applicants by doing an online search for them, and if they come across anything questionable, they will eliminate those applicants from the process.

The final stages of the job application process can trip up Millennials, too. Coach your clients around whom they choose as their references and make sure they ask permission from their references first. Millennials often are not aware of the etiquette around asking for references and keeping them informed during the process.

Seeing Challenges as Opportunities

Millennials face many challenges in the rapidly changing workplace. Each of the pitfalls described above is an opportunity to help your clients navigate the challenging waters of their job search more smoothly with greater self-awareness, self-confidence, and skill. As young adults, Millennials are still figuring out who they are, what they value, and what success means to them. As a coach, you have an incredible opportunity to support and guide them so that they can create a successful, *repeatable* process for finding the next job opportunity that is the right fit for them.

Valerie Dorn (Certified Professional Coach) is founder and owner of Find Fulfillment Coaching. She received a B.S. degree in psychology from the University of Wisconsin, master's degrees in school and professional counseling from the University of Delaware and the University of Pennsylvania, and her Certified Professional Coach training at iPEC (Institute for Professional Excellence in Coaching). With a background in education, counseling, and advising, Valerie, who is also a yoga and meditation teacher, has helped thousands of people achieve their academic, career, and personal goals through her work in higher education and healthcare. To learn more about Valerie, visit her website at: www.valerie-dorn.com.

CHAPTER 2

BUILDING A FOUNDATION OF TRUST

By Leigh Higgins

> *"My coach was able to listen to my ideas, concerns,*
> *and thoughts without judgment. She created*
> *a safe place for me to share with her."*
> —Elizabeth

Trust is an essential element in the coaching relationship—because feeling safe and supported is the dynamic in which breakthroughs occur. A climate of trust allows clients to get to the root of what is in the way of moving forward, allowing them to thrive in whatever they choose to pursue. In this chapter, we will be discussing strategies for developing a sense of trust between coach and clients in their 20s.

Many Millennials are finding themselves out of school, back at home, and unable to get a full-time job with benefits. Their expectations for finding meaningful work are not being met. It is proving a challenge for them to step into the self-sufficient, independent lives they imagined would be waiting for them as young adults. Because this is more difficult than they expected, they are in need of some tools to help them navigate their next steps. It is not the aim of this chapter to discuss *why* that might be the case, but it is their reality. As a consequence, their morale tends to be fragile, and they can be defensive and closed until you are able to connect with them on some level and demonstrate how coaching can help.

For the most part, the clients I have coached have also been unfamiliar with coaching and not necessarily interested in the mechanics of it. All they know is that they need a job and that it's not happening. This is where cultivating trust as a foundational element in the relationship can help.

Meet Your Young Clients Where They Are and Work From There

How do we approach helping these young people, placing trust at the forefront? Normally with new clients, I start by explaining what coaching is and how it can help them. Then I offer some exercises that elicit their values, life purpose, and life vision to help them learn more about who they are, what they want, and where they're headed. With Millennials, however, I have found that the process of defining coaching and having them do the exercises has not engaged them in the same way as older coaching clients. What has been helpful at the start of the relationship is to spend the initial session chatting informally to get to know them, followed by some general but probing questions about what they like and are interested in. This has helped to raise their energy and get them talking.

As we might imagine or remember from our own experience, young people are in a stage of exploration and discovery about what is available to them out in the world. They are looking outward as they seek what the world has to offer them, rather than inward at what they can offer the world. Personal growth, a core part of coaching and the maturation process, is not quite on their radar yet. They are primarily focused on the goal of getting a job and feeling a sense of security and independence, and they don't necessarily see how inner exploration can help with this. So it is important for coaches to be creative in their approach, to look for subtle ways to help them see the impact that this work can have, and to help them build a strong foundation for their future. Some respond with curiosity to the idea of looking inward and some are just not ready yet. So be open to how it unfolds.

How Do We Develop Trust?

Trust can happen relatively quickly or can take time to develop—but in all scenarios it stems from a feeling or an experience of safety.

Confidentiality is an important aspect of the work you will be doing together. When clients trust what they say will not be shared outside of your conversations, the relationship gives the client the opportunity to be authentic and share in ways they may not be able to in most other relationships.

The coach's ability to weave a net of empathy, acceptance, and compassion, together with inspiration and genuine curiosity, allows clients to lower the walls they've built around their heart and remove the masks that do not reflect who they truly are. This is the space where transformation occurs.

The approaches below are applicable to all coaching clients, but these are the ones I have found that go a long way in creating a powerful, mutually trusting relationship with Millennials.

1. Deep listening, offering non-judgmental, emotional support outside of parental support.
2. Committing to them through patience and consistency.

3. Setting boundaries and holding them accountable, but with gentleness. Treating them as adults.
4. Inspiring them, identifying their strengths and gifts, creating energy through possibility and opportunity.
5. Acting as a mentor as well as a coach, connecting clients with others who can help them.
6. Storytelling, offering your perspective, and allowing yourself to be authentic and vulnerable.

These approaches are addressed in more detail below.

1. Deep Listening

There is listening and then there is deep listening—and only the latter is a powerful catalyst for building trust. Ordinary listening generally means that you listen to what someone says and respond with your own idea, based on your own experience, with suggestions for how someone with a completely different life experience "should" move forward. Often we don't really hear what the person is trying to convey. We listen until we think we have a solution, stop listening, wait politely or interrupt the person to share our insight, and wait for them to appreciate us.

In contrast, deep listening requires a level of compassion and an absence of judgment on the coach's part to create a safe space for clients to articulate the complexities of what they are going through. It means digging deeper with follow-up questions that enable both people to gain more clarity as to the root of the issue. Finally, deep listening requires the coach to be able to:

- read the client's emotional state along with what he or she is saying;
- tap into their own intuition to read between the lines;

- mirror back what they have interpreted to see if this resonates with the reality of the situation.

When our clients feel heard, there is no mistaking the experience by either party. You will notice an unmistakable shift in body language and personal energy that demonstrates a true connection has been established. It can run the gamut from a silent, open-mouthed disbelief that you have articulated their experience to an excited outpouring of further details and revelations that have desperately needed to be released. Sometimes I believe I actually saw the light bulb go on over their head.

I have had experiences where I thought I knew what would benefit a client and help her move forward, only to find that what I was attempting to share did not resonate with the client—and was even a distraction from what we were trying to accomplish. It was a clear reminder to me that in coaching it is always and only the client's agenda that matters.

As coaches, we know the importance of a non-judgmental presence. How often do each of us get even an hour a week where someone who is trained to listen gives us their undivided attention, does not judge our situation, and is able to frame empowering questions in a safe space that enables us to discover the answers ourselves? We should all be so lucky.

Tip: Before each session, set an intention to allow your intuition to be the guiding force as you ask empowering questions. When clients feel truly heard and understood, the walls come down and the insights pour forth.

2. Committing to the Client

What does it mean to commit to your Millennial coaching client with the intention of building trust? In addition to creating a sense of safety and meeting clients where they are, it means being a presence in their life that they can rely on, that they can reach out to when they find themselves unable to navigate a situation on their own, and that inspires them to be their best self in all situations.

When we commit to a person or a situation, a sense of trust naturally develops, because that person does not have to be on alert to protect himself from manipulation, abandonment, or betrayal. Strong words, yes, but this is the delicate nature of trust. Importantly, when we are able to foster trust in the coaching relationship, it facilitates the client's ability to see from multiple perspectives and choose the most effective option for his current situation. Commitment also reduces stress and allows for clarity of thinking primarily due to this developing bond of trust. Clear thinking is crucial in moving through and around the obstacles we face in life.

Lastly, commitment in any scenario means that we sometimes go above and beyond what is expected of us. Clients expect professionalism and that the coaches meet their responsibilities as they understand them. But when a coach goes beyond these agreed-upon parameters in ways that are not expected, trust is engendered. To recipients of this generosity, it is not an experience easily forgotten.

I have often extended a session because we were making progress at the end. And from experience I realized that seeing it through to reach an insight or resolution engendered trust in ways that strengthened the emerging bond in the relationship. It moves out of the realm of work to one of seeing others as human beings. When we connect on this human level, trust is the result.

I also offer to be available via email/text and phone if the client needs support between sessions. They don't often take me up on it in the beginning, but there are times where they do reach out. Demonstrating your commitment can be a turning point in the relationship. Learning through experience that you are willing to be there for them softens the often tough exterior that they present and can give them permission to share more deeply, which leads to more successful outcomes for the client.

Tip: In every session reiterate how you are willing to support clients, what they can expect from you, and consistently model for them the commitment you expect them to uphold to you. This will also help them demonstrate this quality to prospective employers.

3. Setting Boundaries and Holding the Client Accountable

Being available for clients outside of the agreed-upon meeting times is a wonderful gift to the client and to the coach as well, because the relationship deepens with shared respect and trust. It also models for the client the example of not just meeting but exceeding expectations and the fruits that come from commitment.

However, it is important to counterbalance this commitment with clear boundaries and guidelines, and to hold the client accountable as a means to foster that shared respect and trust. Open, honest, and clear communication is essential. If the Millennial clients know where you stand, what to expect, and that they will held accountable for their actions, they will likely respond with their own level of commitment to match yours. Boundaries can include punctuality at sessions so your time is not wasted, showing up to sessions prepared and present, and not abusing your offer to connect outside the sessions. Usually, just mentioning they have crossed a line is enough to hold them accountable. But if the situation persists, you can remind them of their agreement to respect these boundaries, and in extreme situations you can end the relationship. I have never had to do this.

Tip: You should have the conversation about boundaries from the start. Otherwise, it can appear that you are not consistent and can undermine trust. Another helpful way to maintain the trust you are building: When a client shows up unprepared, remind them, without judgment, of their commitment, and also explore why they didn't follow through. Possibly some other life event got in the way or their assignment was not the right one for them. At this point you can discuss what got in the way and resolve it so they can be prepared for the next session—or by creating assignments that engage them more deeply.

If they understand they must meet you halfway in their efforts and that you will be accountable to them as well, they usually rise to the occasion. If they don't, it's a perfect learning opportunity for them. As an example, one Millennial client did not respect my boundaries outside of our sessions by texting me incessantly to vent his frustration with a personal issue. I attempted to guide him away from the victim energy he was expressing with strategies for letting it go and opening to new perspectives on his situation. This did not help. I then explained to him how his texts were an inappropriate distraction, taking me away from time with my family. Once he realized that his need to vent was affecting me adversely, he immediately apologized and it was never an issue again. This mutual commitment to each other builds the bond of trust at a foundational level and is rooted in the desire we all have to live up to our responsibilities, whatever our goals may be.

Tip: Hold your Millennial clients accountable by setting the bar high with your expectations of the relationship, but do it with compassion and encouragement while you hold their feet to the fire.

4. Inspiring and Energizing Them
Understanding that the Millennials who come for coaching tend to be dispirited because of their inability to find meaningful work, my

goal for them is to leave the session pumped to do the work we have agreed they would do. If they feel good about themselves, they are more likely to move out of their comfort zones in pursuit of what they want.

Shifting a client's energy into a space of possibility, opportunity, and excitement about their future can often be facilitated by helping them to see, despite their relative inexperience, the intangible as well as demonstrable qualities they have to offer. Often they don't yet have a clear idea of what their strengths and potential contributions are. As professional coaches, we are trained in deep listening to observe personal qualities that often go unnoticed or unacknowledged in our clients.

I ask them to tell me about their work and life experience so I can discover what their strengths are and mirror them back. Often they are surprised and delighted at what I am able to piece together about them from what they have told me. This shift in energy will help them face their job search with renewed enthusiasm and navigate obstacles along the way with more confidence and grace.

For example, one client, whom I was helping to prepare for an interview, was having trouble articulating his strengths and was at a loss. I had only been coaching him for a few sessions but was able to list at least 7-8 qualities that I had noticed he possessed that an employer would value. They resonated with him on some level, and he was able to come up with examples of how he had demonstrated these on previous occasions. He was able to use these examples in his interview and reported back to me that his sense of confidence in himself increased dramatically.

Tip: Inspire them with their own gifts. Here's an excellent way to begin this process: At the end of the first session or as soon as you have a mental picture of your clients, share with them all of the qualities you see in them that reflect their potential and possibility.

And make it a regular part of closing each session. However, do not make up qualities that you do not perceive in your clients. They will not resonate with them, and you will not have modeled the authenticity you want them to express.

5. Acting as Mentor

In the traditional coaching model, coaches are not mentors. We are empowerment and transition specialists. However, young clients generally do not have the extensive networking contacts or work life experience to develop a frame of reference for what they want to do. Or if they do have an idea about what they want, they don't necessarily know the reality of what that work looks like in practice. So, sometimes it is helpful to broaden our role.

One way we can create exposure in this area is to share our own networking connections so that between sessions our clients can reach out to people in the field they are exploring to help them decide if this is where they want to put their energies. I have connected clients with colleagues who have generously offered for the client to visit their office to get a feel for the work. Often though, phone conversations are sufficient to get a flavor for the work and to get an idea if it is a path they want to pursue further. And by being introduced to new people, recent graduates feel more connected to the working world.

What also works well for Millennial clients is for them to seek out friends and colleagues whom they might know in a particular field. It doesn't need to be a first-hand relationship for your client to benefit.

Tip 1: If you don't feel confident that your client will treat this networking connection with the same respect you would, either make it clear that your reputation is on the line or defer this until you feel comfortable your client will follow through. I had an experience in which my client canceled his first appointment at the last minute and was late to the next one he scheduled. When I next spoke to my connection, I could sense his frustration. Prepare your client well so he or she is mindful of the opportunity.

Tip 2: Be flexible about what "coaching" is with young adults. Sometimes we have to wear different hats to facilitate the results our clients are looking for.

6. Storytelling

There is great understanding and healing to be gained from stories. Sharing our stories and listening to others' stories helps us see how we fit in the fabric of life and enables us to start to let go of the fear and obstacles that impede our progress.

Again, in the traditional coaching model we do not generally share much about ourselves in our sessions. But being authentic and displaying our own vulnerability with Millennials is one of the best ways I have found to connect and create a bond of trust with them. This sharing or storytelling allows clients access to scenarios that resemble what they are currently experiencing and helps them imagine themselves emerging from their own situations as stronger and more experienced people. They see that there is a light at the end of the tunnel, that they are not the only ones going through challenges, and that there are multiple perspectives from which they can view their situation. I also encourage them to openly share their own stories. This reciprocal sharing goes a long way in building trust in the relationship.

It is important to not only share your successes but to also share what may have been spectacular blunders on your path. In fact, the stories that didn't end well at the time might be the most effective tool for shifting their understanding of what is possible for them. They begin to see how the cycle of change is inevitable and that their current situation will eventually evolve into something new.

As you share your own stories, the bond of trust grows such that when they begin to share their own stories, they won't tend to censor themselves as much. This enables young people to create a truer mental picture of the situation. They get clarity simply by having to articulate their thoughts and experiences coherently. And finally, they realize the situations they are in are not as life-and-death as they appear, which gives them courage to proceed and lessens the fear associated with how life might turn out for them.

Tip: Give Millennials the gift of sharing yourself authentically.

Trust Leads to Powerful Results

Trust necessarily involves allowing ourselves to be vulnerable with others with the understanding that it is reciprocal, safe, and empowering. By exploring our humanness in this way, we can support each other in living lives full of meaning and purpose.

We have looked at six strategies as opportunities to build trust with Millennial coaching clients. These are by no means the only ways to build trust, but in my experience they are powerful tools that have yielded extraordinary results. By exploring these strategies and experiencing the trust that they engender, clients can begin to confidently create what is next for them with the help of the coach and the coaching process. And you as the coach have the opportunity to learn and grow as well, evolving your coaching toolkit to have an even more powerful impact with another generation.

Coaching is an art as much as a science, and trust is the centerpiece of this relationship. I would encourage you to open to your intuitive nature and see in what direction it leads. Trust yourself to ask the questions that arise spontaneously, however unrelated they may seem. Trust that once clients begin to experience breakthroughs and insights, it will begin to make sense to them that they are an integral part of the co-creative process. Cultivating trust can only lead to richer lives for all of us.

Leigh Higgins (Certified Professional Coach) graduated with a B.A. in economics from Rutgers University and an M.A. in education from the University of London. His coach training was completed at iPEC (Institute for Professional Excellence in Coaching). He specializes in personal growth, shamanic healing practices, life and job transitioning, leadership development, and conflict resolution. He has worked in corporate America for 25+ years. Leigh lives in Hoboken, NJ.

CHAPTER 3

COPING WITH DISCOURAGEMENT, BUILDING SELF-CONFIDENCE

By Cara Maksimow

> *"I was born and raised in public housing, and college was my only time away from it. I actually thought I could escape a life of poverty and violence. I was entirely wrong, and these past three years have shown me that. My wanting a different life for myself and being led to believe it was possible seems like a cruel joke."*
>
> —*Lawrence*

Self-esteem can be a crucial component of any job hunt. For your clients, having confidence in their own abilities and strengths is arguably as important as having the actual skills required for a particular job. Self-confidence and self-esteem will not come through to a prospective employer if they are not genuine. Your clients' actions on a job interview will be guided by their thoughts, emotions, and beliefs about their ability to succeed.

If you are working with Millennials right out of college, it is important to consider the environment they are coming from. During their college career they had been provided a great deal of positive reinforcement, immediate feedback, and support. Life was laid out for them—taking classes, studying, engaging in college social organizations, and receiving specific feedback and guidance from professors were keynotes of their educational experience. Now the time has come to find a career that can utilize their skills and education in a way that they find fulfilling and meaningful. Expectations of success are high. That is when reality can hit them like a ton of bricks. Rejection on this level is new and unexpected. In academia expectations of what to do and how to do it were clearly outlined for them. As career coach Beth Hendler-Grunt, who specializes in helping recent college graduates, has written, "Often, it is just completely overwhelming to step into an environment that has no syllabus, study guide, structure, timetable or set rules. For years our students are clearly told what is expected of them, and now employer expectations are not so clear."

Your clients may have become used to a level of hand-holding, such that when they begin their job search, they're often not prepared for ambiguity and self-guided direction. Job descriptions from prospective employers are often vague or full of jargon, leading graduates to unclear expectations. Following an interview, your clients may receive a generic email stating they were not chosen for the position—if they receive anything back at all. Specific feedback on what was missing or why they were not chosen is almost non-existent. This experience can negatively affect a client's self-esteem and confidence, which may appear to you as a lack of grit or resiliency.

How Grit Affects Self-Confidence

The importance of "grit" is described by Angela Duckworth, a psychologist at the University of Pennsylvania, in her recent book *Grit: The Power of Passion and Perseverance*. Duckworth references studies showing that achievement of difficult goals entails not only talent but also the sustained, focused *application* of talent over time. Having grit showed predictive validity of future success measures beyond IQ. When our clients lose confidence in themselves and their talents, they lose that all-important ability to maintain focus, perseverance, and to make the extraordinary efforts needed to succeed. They are challenged to remain confident and resilient after a string of rejections. Self-esteem, which may have appeared stronger during adolescence and young adulthood, is now affected.

Nathaniel Branden, psychotherapist and founder of the Branden Institute for Self-Esteem, writes on the website www.esteemedself. com:

> *"Self-esteem, fully realized, is the awareness that we are equal to the obstacles placed in front of us. Self-esteem is confidence in our ability to think, confidence in our ability to cope with the basic challenges of life, and confidence in our right to be successful and happy. People with appropriate levels of self-esteem are assured in their right to feel worthy, enjoy the fruits of their efforts, and assert their needs and wants."*

If we apply this definition to our clients, we can see how having poor self-esteem can undermine their ability to find career opportunities that match their skills and passions. (For more on Dr. Branden's methods of building self-esteem, see his book *Six Pillars of Self-Esteem* and his website: Nathanielbranden.com.)

I would like to walk you through an example of a young man I worked with recently. Bob graduated with a degree in sport management. During his college career, Bob had been an excellent student with a high GPA. He also held various leadership positions at his university and was able to find a job directly out of school doing sales and marketing for a small local sports team. He had been working for about a year when he decided to move back to the city where he grew up. This meant finding a new job. Since success had come fairly easily for him the first time, he wasn't very concerned about finding work in the same field in another part of the country. He had repeatedly been given positive feedback and reinforcement; yet he had not fully internalized the confidence needed to withstand repeated rejection that came with his job search.

After a few months of failed attempts at getting a job offer, Bob began to doubt himself and his career choices. He wondered if he had made a mistake with his current career path and questioned his judgment and decision-making. Having always been successful, he had a tendency to be a perfectionist. In other words, he had an expectation of receiving a job offer right away and saw anything less than what he expected as a complete failure. After spending a few months of sending out resumes and getting very little response from prospective employers, he began feeling anxious and defeated. That ultimately hindered his performance on job interviews.

When I started working with Bob, he was doing the "throw everything at the wall to see what sticks" routine. He was spending a fair amount of time randomly scrolling through job openings, unsure of how to narrow his search. His fear about not being able to find a job began to affect his judgment around his own strengths and interests—he felt overwhelmed, without a real focus or plan.

Using Bob as an example, I would like to focus on three concepts and action steps that may be helpful to consider when you are working with your clients on confidence, self-esteem, or grit.

- **Perfectionism**
- **Explanatory Style**
- **Self-Talk**

The Trap of Perfectionism

As a clinical therapist I often see people with symptoms of anxiety and depression rooted in a sense of unrealistic perfectionism. As a coach, I also notice that clients who struggle with self-esteem during their job search often identify themselves as perfectionists. Researcher and writer Brené Brown explains in her book, *The Gifts of Imperfection*, perfectionism is different than we might think.

> *"Perfectionism is not the same thing as striving to be your best. Perfectionism is not about healthy achievement and growth. Perfectionism is the belief that if we live perfect, look perfect, and act perfect we can minimize or avoid the pain of blame, judgment, and shame. Perfectionism is a twenty-ton shield that we lug around thinking it will protect us when, in fact, it's the thing that's really preventing us from taking flight."*

One of the first things I did with Bob was to help him identify unrealistic expectations, which were clouding his judgment. For example, Bob expected that each time he sent a resume and cover letter for a job he really wanted, he would get a callback for an interview. If he believed that the job was a perfect fit, it was hard for him to grasp the fact he did not receive a callback. If he came across a job in his field that looked interesting to him but was not a perfect fit, he hesitated to send out a resume for fear he might get an offer for something he was not certain he wanted to do. Bob and I discussed the importance of moving forward with applying to positions that seemed close to what he wanted to do, even if not exact. He would be able to ask questions and learn more about the role if given the opportunity to interview. I explained that if he did not apply, he wouldn't really know if it could have been a good fit. At one point I asked him to write out the word "Perfection" on a piece of paper, then physically rip it up and throw it away as a symbol of letting it go of unrealistic expectations around his job search.

When you are working with clients who have a tendency toward perfectionism, they can easily become derailed when things do not go according to plan. Helping them to identify their own triggers and let go of unrealistic expectations can refocus your clients away from the idea of "perfect" and toward a healthy and appropriate focus on striving toward realistic career goals. As Gretchen Rubin wrote in *The Happiness Project*, "Don't let the perfect be the enemy of the good."

Explanatory Style and Optimism

Your explanatory style is how you habitually explain to yourself why you experienced a particular event. Explanatory styles can be either largely optimistic or pessimistic, according to University of Pennsylvania's Dr. Martin E. Seligman, who is considered to be the "father of Positive Psychology." In general an optimistic explanatory style is associated with positive mood and good morale, while a pessimistic style can be associated with symptoms of depression and helplessness. In his book *Learned Optimism*, Dr. Seligman describes three crucial dimensions of explanatory style. Let's look at each one as it relates to Bob.

Permanence: When Bob told himself he would "never" find a job he liked, he was seeing the situation as permanent. For a pessimist, bad events persist while positive events are seen as temporary. Being caught in the weeds, he was unable to see the clearing that would eventually come up for him.

Personalization: Feeling frustrated, Bob began to believe he was not qualified or capable of finding a job. He started to question his capabilities unrealistically and blamed himself for things that were outside of his control. Pessimists attribute negative events internally and positive events externally, while optimists do the opposite.

Pervasiveness: After receiving a rejection email following an interview he felt good about, Bob told me that he thought it was pointless to pursue similar jobs and started to feel discouraged in other areas of his life as well. He saw a failure as universal instead of specific to that particular situation.

When working with your clients, listen in session for how they use these three explanatory styles from the perspective of optimism or pessimism. You can help them identify where they fall within these three elements of explanatory style and bring a different perspective to the situation. Dr. Seligman offers a test people can take in order to score their level of optimism in *Learned Optimism* (p. 33) or online at AuthenticHappiness.com (https://www.authentichappiness.sas.upenn.edu/testcenter). To take the test, it is necessary to sign in and create a password. This test can help you and your clients get a better understanding of their baseline of optimism versus pessimism.

Exercises to Increase Optimism

Tools that can be used with clients to increase optimism and positivity have been established in the positive psychology field. Positive Psychology researcher Dr. Sonja Lyubomirsky has shown that 40% of our overall happiness can influenced by "intentional activity." That means we are able to increase our level of optimism through positive psychology exercises aimed at noticing the good in our lives.

One simple tool is to keep a gratitude journal. Ask your clients to identify three to five things they noticed about their day for which they were grateful. The list does not need to be full of major events, but simply things that they identify as positive throughout the day.

Another exercise could be to write a "thank you" letter. Ask your client to write a letter to someone they believe has helped them in the past. You want them to write specifically about why that person's actions were meaningful. Going a step further, your client could deliver the letter and pay a visit to the person, if possible. Expressing gratitude and doing something for others are powerful ways to increase joy and positive emotion, which lead to increased optimism and self-esteem.

Using Self-Talk to Cope with Discouragement

While explanatory style describes where people fall on the three dimensions listed above, self-talk is the actual inner dialogue we have with ourselves as a result of a situation. Our self-talk is often automatic and happens at a subconscious level. It can be positive and productive, or negative and destructive. Young clients faced with repeated discouragement may exhibit a stronger negative bias toward themselves, which lessens objectivity and resilience and ultimately hurts their job search. The more your client focuses attention on his failings, the more he sees them. It becomes a self-fulfilling prophecy.

Self-talk is vulnerable to inaccurate thoughts that can negatively affect how we feel and respond. Psychiatrist Aaron T. Beck, who developed the system of cognitive behavioral therapy, called these self-defeating thoughts "cognitive distortions." When working with your clients, you'll want to keep an eye on some of the more common cognitive distortions that come up and help your client identify new and more productive self-talk. Here are examples of some of the distortions and what you can do to help your client with each one:

Filtering: Taking the negative details and magnifying them while filtering out all positive aspects of a situation. For example, your client may come away from a job interview focusing on the one question he or she was not prepared for. Help your client to replay the interview and identify and evaluate all responses more objectively in order to prepare for next opportunity.

In my work with Bob, I noticed he often started our session by filling me in on examples of where he had *not* made progress over the past week. I needed to redirect him toward a focus on what he *had* accomplished and small wins he had overlooked.

Polarized Thinking: Things are either "black or white" with no middle ground. Your client may view her performance that is less than perfect as a total failure. In this situation it is helpful to help her see shades of gray in the situation and areas of improvement, as well as areas where she's doing well in her job search.

Overgeneralization: Similar to the idea of permanence, in which it can be difficult to see a light at the end of a tunnel, overgeneralization is the thought that if something bad happens only once, we expect it to happen over and over again. The first rejection can lead your client to assume that each subsequent attempt will be met with the same response. You want to help your client see that one outcome does not dictate future outcomes. When working with Bob, I asked him to examine the evidence for this false belief. This helped him gain insight into where he could adjust his thinking and see the situation from a more balanced perspective.

Emotional Reasoning: When we believe that what we feel must automatically be true, we are reasoning with our emotions. If your client *feels* stupid or defeated, then he begins to believe he must *be* stupid and unqualified. He is allowing the unhealthy emotions that he's feeling define who he is as a person. When you hear your client using emotional reasoning, help him to identify it and take a more realistic perspective on the situation.

All these modes of inaccurate thinking result in negative self-talk. Here are some common examples of negative self-talk and ways to reframe them to a more realistic and positive thoughts.

HOW TO REFRAME
NEGATIVE SELF-TALK

Negative Self-Talk	More Realistic Reframing
I do horribly at interviews! That's why I did not get called back for a second round of interviews with that job.	If I review the interview in my head, I recognize a couple of questions I could have answered differently. Next time I will be more prepared for those questions.
I don't have a chance at that type of role—that job is well over my head, and I will never be able to get there.	My skills and experience may not be a fit for one particular role in that industry. However, I can explore a more entry-level position that can help me get the experience needed to revisit that role in a few years.
I met the job requirements, but they hired someone else. Nothing good ever happens to me!	This last employer may have had a more qualified candidate for the role. However, that does not mean I am not going to find a good fit for me next time.
I am never going to get a "real" job, I am going to be stuck at my part-time job forever.	I am growing and learning problem-solving and other skills in my current part-time job that can help me in future full-time career opportunities. How can I translate those skills for my next job interview?
Because I don't have an Ivy League education, I am limited in the types of jobs I can realistically apply for.	Employers look for well-rounded candidates with varying experiences and education, and my education can absolutely allow me many opportunities.
I don't have any "good" connections. Most good jobs are about who you know.	If I take a look at my network and start connecting more with people on LinkedIn, I bet I will find I know people in places I had not realized.

When helping your client reframe his or her self-talk, it can also be helpful to point out that everyone experiences setbacks in their lives at one point or another. This can provide comfort and allow for self-compassion and self-appreciation in your clients' newly reframed self-talk. In her book *Self-Compassion: The Proven Power of Being Kind To Yourself*, Kristen Neff, Ph.D., of the University of Texas at Austin, discusses the act of softening our critical voice by imagining we were giving advice to a very close friend. Ask your client to reframe his or her self-talk as if he or she were providing positive and kind advice to someone they care for. That new self-talk will most likely have more warmth, compassion, and empathy.

When working with Bob, I was able to help him recognize and subsequently reframe his thoughts more realistically and appropriately moving forward. This helped him feel more confident that despite setbacks during the process, he would find a role that was a good fit for him. When Bob was able to recognize that the negative thoughts he was having were just thoughts and not truths, and that he had the ability to reframe his thoughts, he was then able to present with more confidence and grit despite rejections along the way. Ultimately he was able to find a job in his field of sports management. He sent me a note a few months later letting me know how much he was enjoying his position and how often he practiced what we had worked on together when faced with challenges in the new job.

Finally, you want to help your clients to identify what is working and going well throughout the job search. It will take conscious efforts to help them see some of the progress that they have made, especially when they have had a string of rejections. When you ask your clients how their week has gone, they will usually begin with the negative and not necessarily describe their wins or accomplishments. By asking them to tell you what went well and where they have had success, you can help them to recognize their progress with less self-criticism and more self-acceptance. Here is an exercise I created to help my clients focus on the positive, which can help reinforce what is going well with their search.

Fill Your Bag with Happiness Exercise: Have your client imagine having a bag that collects negative experiences, frustrations, and emotions throughout the day. Visualize emptying the contents of the bag out and refilling it with answers to three questions whose initials spell out the word BAG.

- What was the **Best** or **Brightest** part of the day?
- What did you **Accomplish**?
- What are you **Grateful** for and why?

The idea is that we are more likely to notice what we spend time thinking about. For example, have you ever noticed that when you start looking to buy a new car all of a sudden you notice that make and model everywhere? That is the same idea. By asking your clients to focus on the wins and the positive, they are more likely to recognize and notice any wins and positives that happen. (More information on *Fill Your BAG Happy* can be found at website www.maximize-wellness.com/bag.html)

When you are working with Millennial clients, keep in mind that you may find yourself in emotionally difficult waters. It can be helpful to have a clinical therapist or psychologist you can check in with to help you identify when discouragement goes beyond an understandable and temporary response to a challenging situation into signs of clinical depression or anxiety, in which case a referral may be appropriate.

In conclusion, while self-esteem can be negatively affected by external circumstances, you can help your young clients build up internal compassion and confidence during your work together. Your support and coaching can provide them with the tools to take into the next phase of their careers to confidently and compassionately persevere through any future challenges they may face.

Cara Maksimow, LCSW, CPC, graduated from Rutgers University with her B.A. in psychology and from Columbia University Graduate School with her master's in clinical social work. In 2014 she founded Maximize Wellness Counseling and Coaching, LLC in NJ, providing counseling and coaching services such as Clinical Psychotherapy, Life Coaching, and Wellness Workshops. She is the author of the book *Lose That Mommy Guilt, Tales and Tips from an Imperfect Mom.* Prior to opening her therapy practice she worked for many years as a pharmaceutical sales trainer and district manager. To learn more visit her website at: www.maximize-wellness.com.

CHAPTER 4

CREATING A LIFE VISION

By Annette Cataldi

> *"Working with [my coach] has been a transformative experience. She approached my career difficulties holistically. I remember she said that it's not about what you do as a career so much as who you want to be. My whole life has improved—finding a career path has been a side effect."*
> —ADAM

"If only I had known then what I know now...." How many times have we heard this old adage? Coaches do not have a crystal ball to predict the future, but they do act as a mirror to reflect the values and motivators of clients to help them embark upon their future with intention.

Most people in mid-to-late career say that they did not plan the path their career took; many times they had intended to go a different direction. Somewhere along the way, though—and often right at the outset—they diverged from their desired path. They accepted opportunities and promotions without taking the time to reflect upon how those choices would impact their career and life goals.

Millennials may face some difficulties as they begin their careers; yet this could turn out to be an important occasion for growth. It all begins with changing their paradigm from viewing a bumpy career start as a struggle to seeing it as an opportunity to launch their career with the greatest gift of all—*vision*.

A young client of mine who was a recent graduate was struggling to find a job. Although very bright and gifted, especially in technology, he felt downtrodden and hopeless. He was distrustful of corporate America and was unwilling to engage with it in any way. Through coaching, he took a deep dive into the life vision he hoped to achieve and the values he held sacred. He was able to see how he could not only benefit personally from engaging—he could be a catalyst for change. This establishment of the "why" for his journey brought him hope and an opportunity to choose his path wisely. Understanding not only *what* we want to do, but *why* we want to do it, takes the journey to a deeper, much more satisfying level and allows for far greater happiness in our lives. He was able to change his perspective from a short-term vision of what he did not want to a long-term vision of what he *did* want. Then he was able to move ahead.

Vision is a word that can evoke an array of thoughts and feelings—from the basic sense of sight to a much deeper sense of purpose driven by one's desires and values. Tapping into the latter can have a profound and life-changing impact, and it can be done with the use of one simple word: *thought*. Careful attention and consideration placed on the things that mean the most to us can bring joy, freedom, and choice into our life. Coaches and mentors of Millennials have the opportunity to bring the gift of vision to their clients.

A **Life Vision** is a desired outcome for one's life. It is a driving force, aligned with personal values and desires, that provides direction and clarity for choices and propels us toward our ultimate goal. Creating a life vision is achieved through a process of deep thought and reflection to determine values, aspirations, motivators, strengths, and goals.

Putting the Grad in the Driver's Seat

Once trust is established between the client and coach and the roles of the coaching relationship have been defined, the coach can begin to facilitate the creation of a life vision. This starts with a clear understanding of the client's expectation for the coaching engagement. Having clients clearly define *what success looks like to them* provides a foundation from which to build. Millennials, who have less experience due to their age, often feel that they are not in control and have to defer to others. These questions put them in the driver's seat and allow them the opportunity to determine the direction of the coaching.

<u>Questions to Clarify Goals for the Coaching Engagement</u>
Listen for areas of confusion, frustration, and concern.

- What brought you here?
- What are your expectations?
- What do you really want?
- If the coaching engagement is successful, what will you be taking away?

With the expectations for the engagement defined, the coach can begin to explore the bigger picture and create awareness that will drive the client's life vision. Most people have given little if any thought to their life vision or how they will go about achieving it. Articulating these things is often very difficult. Coaches have two main tools to discern a client's underlying drivers: career/personality assessments and powerful questions.

Through the use of these tools, a coach can begin to uncover core values and bring awareness to the client's greatest motivators. The more self-knowledge young people attain as to why they do the things they do, what energizes and depletes them, what they like to do, and what they are good at doing—the easier it is for them to make decisions that are in alignment with their values and the more satisfied, engaged, and empowered they will feel. With self-knowledge, Millennials can begin their careers intentionally, on a road of their choosing, to a place they want to go.

Assessment Tools

Assessments can be used to complement thought-provoking questions to create deeper awareness and provide a foundation for discussion. Assessment results may provide a significant source of awareness that the client might otherwise not realize regarding their motivators, strengths, work preferences, emotional drivers, etc.

One client who was just beginning her career in social work, which had been her major field in college, did not understand why she felt stressed and unhappy at work. Through the use of a strengths-based assessment, it became evident that her preferred approach was deliberative. She was careful in life to reduce risks, and the unpredictable nature of social work was causing her a great deal of stress. The field of social work was forcing the client into an environment that was fundamentally contrary to her strengths. While the client had an idea of the inherent disconnect, the black-and-white assessment results were the impetus for her to actually make a change. In addition, the assessment confirmed her strengths for an alternative field that she was considering.

There are a plethora of assessment tools, all providing a unique insight and perspective. The coach will need to decide if employing one of these tools will be useful to bring the client clarity in a specific area.

The following are two assessment tools that are widely used and have withstood the test of time. StrengthsFinder ® focuses on what the client does well and builds on that. This assessment, which can be taken online in coordination with the book *StrengthsFinder 2.0*, by Tom Rath, provides a strong foundation for decision-making. The book *What Color is Your Parachute*, by Richard N. Bolles, also contains a great assessment for identifying career options. It focuses on personality traits that align with certain professions. Although this book has been around for many years, it is updated regularly to provide current and relevant data.

Asking Powerful Questions

Though assessment tools can provide useful information, the coach's primary tool in helping young people discover their desired path is the use of powerful questions. These probing questions, which cannot be answered by a simple "yes" or "no," require grads to dig deep and reflect upon aspects of their life and character that they may not have considered.

To assist clients in creating a Life Vision, the coach can guide them through the following steps to identify the path that is right for them.

Six Steps to Creating a Life Vision:

1. Clarify Career Aspirations
2. Understand Motivators
3. Identify Strengths
4. Uncover Values
5. Craft a Life Mantra and Vision Statement
6. Determine Goals

1. Clarify Career Aspirations

It is important to begin with clarifying the reasons for the client's academic degree and career choice. The client's degree may or may not be in alignment with what they actually want to do.

Questions to Clarify Career Aspirations:

Note: Listen for realistic expectations. Determine if more research is necessary to understand the typical career trajectory for their field of choice. Identify motivation for choices.

- Why did you choose your degree/field of study?
- What do you want your career to look like a year from now? 5 years? 10 years?
- Upon completion of your degree, do you remain happy with your choice?
- If there were no obstacles to achieving any career, would you choose differently?
- What was the most important thing you learned about your major while pursuing it that you did not expect?
- How does that impact your desire to pursue this career?

2. Understand Motivators

Career choices are often made on the basis of motivators that are only temporary, such as pay. It is important to ascertain what motivators sustain the client. Due to their youth, Millennials, unlike more experienced clients, may also rely on motivators that are driven by their parents. This tends to be a sensitive issue, and often they may not even be cognizant that their parents' beliefs are an underlying reason for their choices. While this is not necessarily negative, it is important that they at least recognize it, so that they may discern if the motivators are real for them. One client's responses were so embedded in his parents' expectations that there needed to be much probing for answers and reasoning before he realized that those things that motivated his parents were in actuality not motivators for him.

Questions to Understand Motivators:
Note: Listen for common themes and skills clients are using when they feel at their best. Understand what is behind the joy and energy that drives their goals. Pay careful attention to the client's voice intonation, animation, passion, and excitement level.

- When in the last 90 days did you feel at your best?
- What was it about those times that made you feel good?
- What are your interests?
- Where do you like to spend your free time?
- In a perfect world, where would you spend your time?
- What brings you the most joy, fills you with energy?
- What depletes you of energy?

3. Identify Strengths
While looking for a client's strengths, it is equally important to understand their greatest challenges. Clarifying both helps to add depth and an understanding of their parameters.

Note: Listen for not only what they are good at doing but what they enjoy doing.

Questions to Identify Strengths:

- What accomplishments are you most proud of thus far? Why?

- What would those who know you best say are your greatest accomplishments?
- What are you best at doing?
- What do others see as your greatest attributes?
- What aspect of college came most naturally to you?
- What areas are most challenging for you?
- What do you find most difficult about searching for a job? Easiest?
- What do your friends commonly ask you to help them do?

4. Uncover Values

Values are at the core of the client's thinking. They go much deeper than aspirations, strengths, and motivators. They are a personal code of ethics that drive thought, decisions, and actions.

Questions to Uncover Values:
Note: *Listen for intensity of emotion and how deeply rooted something is.*

- What is most important to you?
- What is currently driving your decisions?
- What values are currently guiding your life?
- What values do you want to guide your life?
- What accomplishments do you want to define you?
- What word do you want people to use to describe you?
- What are you most passionate about?
- What unique qualities do you value most about yourself?
- How can using your unique qualities make an impact on others?
- What legacy do you want to leave?
- As you reach the twilight of your life, what do you want to have achieved? Why? What will that look like?

Exercise to Identify Core Values:

1. Have the clients begin by circling 15 words that resonate for them from the **Values Identification** list on the next page.
2. Have them review the circled words and look for similarities or themes, and if possible have them identify one word that can incorporate the others.
3. Have them reduce their list to 5 core values that truly identify who they are.
4. Refer to these core values as a guide in assisting them to make decisions and/or choices.
5. Challenge them to base their actions in accordance with these values.

5. Craft a Life Mantra and Vision Statement

The "coach's mirror" is most effective in reflecting the aspirations, motivations, strengths, and values back to Millennials so that they have a true picture of themselves. As clients try to discern their vision, the coach challenges their thinking by asking them if it is in alignment with their stated values, aspirations, motivators, strengths, and goals. This questioning helps the client remain focused and intentionally choose a path that will be satisfying and fulfilling. Their *vision statement* is a direct reflection of who they are and what is important to them and what they hope to achieve by living their life in accordance with their values and aspirations. One vision statement a client wrote was, "Live life by being fully present in each moment."

The *life mantra* is a short phrase that they use as a reminder of their vision and how they will go about achieving it, e.g. "Enjoy the ride." Once the vision statement and mantra have been determined,

VALUES IDENTIFICATION

Acceptance	Enthusiasm	Intelligence	Professionalism
Accomplishment	Entrepreneurship	Intuitiveness	Punctuality
Adventure	Equality	Justice	Purpose
Affection	Excellence	Kindness	Recognition
Appreciation	Excitement	Knowledge	Recreation
Authenticity	Exhilaration	Leadership	Reflection
Balance	Expertise	Leading	Relationships
Beauty	Fame	Learning	Relaxation
Being the Best	Family	Listening	Respectfulness
Belonging	Fitness	Love	Rest
Catalyzing	Flexibility	Loyalty	Risk
Challenge	Formality	Mastery	Romance
Change	Freedom	Meaning	Safety
Charitableness	Friendship	Motivation	Security
Cheerfulness	Fun	Mystery	Self-Awareness
Comfort	Future Focus	Nature	Selflessness
Communication	Giving	Nurturing	Sense of Humor
Community	Gratitude	Optimism	Sharing
Compassion	Happiness	Organization	Simplicity
Competition	Hard Work	Partnership	Sincerity
Connection	Health	Passion	Solitude
Control	Honesty	Patience	Spirituality
Courage	Honor	Peacefulness	Status
Creativity	Humility	Perfection	Synergy
Curiosity	Humor	Perseverance	Teamwork
Discovery	Impacting	Persuasiveness	Thought
Educate	Independence	Popularity	Tradition
Education	Individuality	Positivity	Truthfulness
Empathy	Influence	Power	Uniqueness
Empowerment	Informality	Pride	Vision
Engagement	Innovation	Privacy	Wealth
Enjoyment	Inspiring	Proactivity	Winning
Entertainment	Integrity	Productivity	Wisdom

encourage the client to write these down and place them somewhere as a constant reminder of what is truly important to them. Having them use these as touch points throughout their lives is powerful. These can be carried in their wallet or printed and placed in a frame.

Questions to Craft the Life Mantra and Vision Statement:

- What short saying would give you daily inspiration?
- What words resonate for you and help to keep you directed?
- Based upon all the soul-searching you have done, what *vision statement* do you want to guide your life?

6. Determine Goals

Armed with their newly gained self-knowledge, clients can begin on their path to attaining their vision. This is done through a continuous process of setting and achieving goals. Goals help the client to break down monumental aspirations into manageable tasks and help them maintain momentum and a positive outlook. The following process provides a framework for goal-setting.

Set the Bar:	Write the top 3 to 5 goals you want to accomplish. These need to be measurable, attainable, and in alignment with your values.
Imagine the Results:	Picture yourself once you have achieved them. Describe how the achievement of each goal would make you feel and/ or how it would change your life.

Acknowledge the Barriers: Determine the obstacles that are likely to get in your way of achieving these goals.

Identify Reinforcements: List all of the people and resources that can help you attain your goal and/or things you can do to remove the barriers.

Create Steps: Break down your goals into smaller tasks that will eventually lead to full achievement.

Chart Progress: Chart how you are doing. List even small successes.

Celebrate: Write exactly what you will do to reward yourself once a goal has been achieved.

Funnel Vision, not Tunnel Vision

Tunnel Vision is limiting, but Funnel Vision is boundless. Items placed into a funnel all go in the same direction. Similarly, when aspirations, motivators, strengths, values, and goals are intentionally brought together, they too all go in the same direction: *toward a **Life Vision***. When these factors are working together, the opportunities for great satisfaction, success, joy, and contentment are boundless. The power of thought at the start of one's career has the force to propel the client to far greater achievements with far more happiness in the long term. That is the gift of vision.

Annette Cataldi is the President of VLV Coaching & Consulting Services, LLC a professional services firm specializing in leadership development and strategic vision. She has more than 15 years of progressive corporate management experience and extensive experience in strategy development and implementation, organization development, and culture assimilation. Prior to becoming an executive coach she was a VP of Human Resources for a Fortune 200 Company with responsibility for more than 50 plants worldwide. Annette holds a master's degree in administration and a bachelor's in business administration. She received her coach training from Coach University. Annette lives in Grosse Pointe, Michigan. To learn more about her coaching practice, visit her website at: www.vlvcoaching.com.

CHAPTER 5

DEFINING THE COACHING RELATIONSHIP

By Mary Kay Wedel

> *"Since graduating I have pretty much drifted through life*
> *and have been unemployed for an extended period of time*
> *(although I have had some short-term jobs). I have no direction,*
> *no real sense of purpose, and am going nowhere fast."*
> —PAUL

The young man had been out of college for five years, and his note touched my heart. Paul had majored in philosophy at Rutgers University and initially thought that he might want to be a lawyer. He received a certificate as a paralegal, but the legal jobs he worked at in this field convinced him not to pursue a law career. Paul was living with his parents, neither of whom had been unemployed and couldn't relate to Paul's situation. Although supportive of their son, they were disappointed that he kept changing jobs and lacked direction in his career. Paul shared, "My parents place constant pressure on me to get a job and stick with it. But they don't realize how hard it is to get hired in anything, much less something I'd like to do."

Paul reached out to Grad Life Choices, the pro bono coaching program for which I volunteer. The program's organizers thought Paul would be a good match for me because of my broad business background and the fact that I too was a Rutgers alum.

I agreed to give Paul 12 sessions on a pro bono basis. Like the other grads I had coached through Grad Life Choices, Paul was looking for career guidance. But I knew he also needed emotional support to deal with his lack of self-confidence along with his doubts and fears.

When graduates seek out coaching, most often they are struggling with starting their career or contending with a career that has been derailed by something (a negative work experience, a bout of illness, a family crisis, the discovery that they really have no interest in the field). Like many young people, they may have dreamed of changing the world—but now their lives are full of frustration and even despair. Unemployed Millennials may be feeling stress, uncertainty, and concern about when and how they will get a job and/or start their career. Lack of income and moving back in with their parents are often their new reality.

Paul's perspective starting out was hopeful. Like most young college grads, he had never worked with a coach before, and he believed that in some vague way coaching would help him find a job. It is the responsibility of the coach to be sure that grads like Paul understand what coaching will mean for them. In addition to establishing a personal connection with the Millennial client, as discussed in Chapter 2 (Building a Foundation of Trust), the coach begins the process with two specific goals: to provide an understanding of coaching and to develop an accountability framework.

Goal 1: Providing an Understanding of Coaching

Since grads have not experienced coaching before, the concept may be unclear and confusing. They are not sure how they can benefit. So the initial meeting is the place to provide the grad with an understanding of coaching. Here are a few brief explanations coaches have used:

"Coaching provides a supportive relationship that helps you achieve your goals."

"Coaching is a conversation without judgment."

"Coaching is about you."

"It's a two-way dialogue designed to discover what's needed and help you take action."

"Coaching is not therapy or counseling."

"Coaching is not a job-finding service."

"Coaching offers a way for you to be accountable for your progress."

Explaining the process in more depth.

Along with the goal of "getting a job," the coach can explain that coaching offers young people a way to assess the things that are really important to them personally and professionally. Coaching can help them learn how to manage their career and increase their odds of getting more of what they want—and less of what they do not want—in their work life. Coaching can inspire and motivate them, and increase their self-esteem and confidence, as well as providing direction and resources, all in a non-judging environment. Coaching can provide perspective in understanding that a "career" is a series of work experiences, and that in the course of each experience the individual is responsible for developing and broadening his or her own skills and capabilities.

Effective coaching conversations require a coach to exercise a highly developed openness to listening. The coach's responsibility is to help clients stay the course, see themselves clearly, and lead them in the direction of uncovering the right decisions and actions themselves. As an experienced adult, you can also be a source of information and connections that will enable them to market themselves more effectively.

Graduates need to have a realistic view of the level of proficiency required to move their career in a specific direction. The coach's role is to ensure that the grad understands that he or she is accountable for his/her own career and that it can and will take an immense amount of personal effort, persistence, motivation, and, in some cases, significant changes to achieve what is desired.

Coaches try to help the grads arrive at authentic and lasting decisions by helping them uncover their values, passions and talents. The process requires the young people to search deep inside themselves. It is facilitated by the coach who asks probing questions and helps the grad work through their answers. These answers can then be used in working out a career plan to enable the grad to choose an appropriate career field, strategize the job search, and access resources available to implement it. Coaches can offer perspective, wisdom, and reference points based on their own professional background and experience. But a coach will not tell a client what to do.

As coaches, it is important for us to not quickly dismiss a grad's aspirations as "unrealistic," but to balance a reality check with support and belief in the grad's potential. The coach can help clients recognize the skills they have and the skills that they need to develop further.

Your belief in and support of your young clients' dreams and desires can be the spark they need to achieve what they didn't initially believe was possible. Oftentimes, this is the most gratifying part of your role as coach.

Readiness Quiz

Not all prospective young clients are ready for coaching. If a Millennial client is to get anything out of coaching, he or she must be willing to make a real effort. For unlike career counseling, which many grads have received at college, coaching involves searching deep inside for answers to very tough, personal questions. The theory is that if the answers come from the client, they will be more authentic and have staying power. Coaching is for individuals who are emotionally and psychologically healthy and who want to make changes and move forward in their lives. What follows is a Readiness Quiz that you can provide to your Millennial client. Along with a serious discussion of the Coaching Contract (discussed and provided later), this readiness quiz can help you and your new client think through whether coaching would be helpful at this time.

Are You Ready for Coaching?

For each question, the client should respond "Agree," "Maybe," or "Disagree."

I am clear as to why I need coaching.
AGREE   MAYBE   DISAGREE

I will get to coaching appointments on time, prepared to work.
AGREE   MAYBE   DISAGREE

I will complete weekly assignments agreed upon with my coach.
AGREE   MAYBE   DISAGREE

I will always be honest with my coach.
AGREE   MAYBE   DISAGREE

I am able to ask for what I need.
AGREE   MAYBE   DISAGREE

I am open-minded concerning alternatives suggested by others.
AGREE   MAYBE   DISAGREE

I am capable of letting go of destructive behavior.
AGREE   MAYBE   DISAGREE

For the most part, I see the glass as half full rather than half empty.
AGREE   MAYBE   DISAGREE

I have realistic expectations concerning my coaching prospects.
AGREE   MAYBE   DISAGREE

I usually seek out support when I need it.
AGREE   MAYBE   DISAGREE

I focus on the future more than on the past.
AGREE   MAYBE   DISAGREE

I generally learn from my mistakes.
AGREE   MAYBE   DISAGREE

I am capable of being fully present, free of distractions, at coaching sessions.
AGREE   MAYBE   DISAGREE

I am the kind of person who hates to give up.
AGREE   MAYBE   DISAGREE

I am willing to take significant risks to improve my life.
AGREE   MAYBE   DISAGREE

Calculate the score by assigning 2 points for Agree, 1 point for Maybe, and 0 points for Disagree. If the prospective client scores less than 15 points, he or she may not a good candidate for coaching at this time. Discuss with clients the answers that indicate a lack of readiness and whether they can be conscious of and work on areas that might interfere with their progress.

Goal 2: Developing an Accountability Framework

The first meeting is also the time to provide a clear understanding of the working relationship between the coach and client and how you will be accountable to each other. This involves six elements:

1. Objectives and boundaries
2. Confidentiality
3. Commitment
4. Uncovering any initial concerns
5. Coaching procedures
6. Agreement on success measures

Let's take a look at these elements in more detail.

1. Objectives and boundaries

Through an initial conversation, the coach will have a sense of the objective the young person is seeking. Together, the coach and the grad design the program to meet the client's needs. Basics such as establishing a set time to talk each week, how many emails and phone call requests are permitted, are items to discuss and for which you should set acceptable boundaries.

> One coach shared: "Although an objective is set, I stay flexible with each session and allow the conversation to be fluid, recognizing that priorities and visions can change through the 12 weeks of coaching."

2. Confidentiality

The coaching relationship is built on trust. The coach agrees to keep all conversations and information with the client private and confidential. Unless the grad reveals that he is a danger to himself or others, no personal ideas, information, or thoughts expressed will be shared with anyone, except with the permission of the client.

3. Commitment

Coaching is an ongoing relationship between a coach and a client. By entering into the relationship, they acknowledge that the client wants to make significant progress and change in his or her life toward career goals. The young person's responsibility is to come to each session on time with no distractions and being truly present and ready to engage in the process. Coaching is a structure that facilitates the process of personal and professional development. The graduate and coach agree that the coaching relationship will be designed together to meet the needs of the client. By entering this relationship, the coach and client acknowledge that the graduate wants to make significant progress and change in his/her life toward career goals. Because progress and change happen at rates unique to each individual, the coach and grad commit to working with each other as indicated in the "coaching procedures" and "agreement on success measures" sections below.

4. Uncovering any initial concerns

The first meeting is the time to answer any questions and concerns about the process. It is also important to share that at any time the grad believes the coaching is not working, he or she should communicate directly with the coach and both will take action to remedy the situation.

5. Coaching procedures

Coaching procedures are established in the Coaching Contract so that everyone understands the ground rules for the coaching relationship.

This is particularly important when working with Millennials, who may never have been involved in a professional services relationship. Some of the concepts that one can generally take for granted with older clients need to be discussed and underscored with young adults in their 20's. Among other things, this would include the length of each session, starting and finishing the session on time, agreement as to how and when to appropriately cancel a scheduled session, and consequences for failure to properly cancel a session that can't be attended. Generally, 24 hours or more are required to change an appointment. Decide how the rescheduling should be requested—i.e., phone, text, or email? How will the sessions themselves be conducted? In person? By phone? Using Skype? Who will make the call?

A number of coaches permit the grad to email the coach between sessions. Establish if phone calls can be made between scheduled appointments and agree to the length of time; e.g., the parties agree to keep the calls to five minutes or less.

6. Agreement on success measures

For most young clients, the goal is to get a job that hopefully starts their career on a more successful track than they have experienced so far. Since the process of getting a job can take considerably more time than three months of coaching, a more realistic tactical outcome for a time-limited coaching engagement might be for grads to: 1. understand the process and steps needed for an effective job search; 2. narrow down the desired field and job roles; and 3. actively go on interviews. In addition, there might be agreement on less tangible but equally important goals, such as improvements in self-understanding and self-confidence. For instance, at the end of the Grad Life Choices program in a follow-up survey, 90% of grads responded, "I feel better about myself."

If self-understanding and self-confidence are goals of the coaching, determine together with your Millennial client some ways in which these can be measured. For instance, for a grad who only makes computer contact in job searching, a willingness to go to a specified number of in-person networking events might be a measurable successful outcome.

The Coaching Contract

In most coaching environments, a coach will provide a coaching contract to the client. This is a formal document that spells out the terms of the coaching engagement and the finances/costs the client will incur. In the case of a not-for-profit arrangement like Grad Life Choices, it is not necessary to include fees. But most coaches still find it important to clearly outline the commitment and responsibilities of both the grad and the coach through a written document. The contract should be discussed carefully with the client and provide opportunities for changes and additions based upon the client's input.

With or without a signed, written agreement, contracting is important at the start of any coaching relationship because it sets the scene in terms of expectations, boundaries, and outcomes. For many Millennials, coaching is their first experience with this type of professional relationship, so clarifying the expectations and responsibilities is especially important. It may feel quite formal, but the experience of coaches is that it provides for better long-term results and commitment.

Below is a sample contract to help set the expectations of the coach and the young client. It is one example of an agreement and not intended to be the only type of agreement used.

Below is a sample coaching agreement, which can be adapted to meet each coach's particular situation and needs. If the coaching is pro bono, don't include the fees.

COACHING
AGREEMENT

CLIENT'S NAME _____

    ADDRESS _____

    EMAIL _____ CELLPHONE _____

COACH'S NAME _____

    ADDRESS _____

    EMAIL _____ CELLPHONE _____

SESSION(S) _____ PER MONTH

FEE $_____ PER MONTH

COACHING COMMITMENT _____ MONTHS

1. I understand that coaching is a professional, facilitating relationship whose purpose is to help me create and achieve goals through developing and implementing a plan suitable to my purposes.

2. I understand that I am responsible for the results of my coaching, which are not guaranteed.

3. I can expect that you, as my coach, will be open and honest and will actively listen to my concerns, challenge me to expand my personal development, and be committed to my success.

4. If I am uncomfortable with the direction of my coaching sessions, I will communicate this to my coach. If I am dissatisfied with the coaching, I can discontinue my sessions at any time.

5. I understand the coaching is not a form of or substitute for mental health treatment, and I will seek such treatment if and when it is necessary. If I am currently being treated by a mental health professional, I have consulted with him/her regarding whether it is advisable for me to work with a coach.

5. If I need professional assistance outside the realm of coaching (e.g., medical, financial, legal, etc.), I will seek such guidance from the appropriate professional.

6. All information at the sessions is confidential and will not be repeated except as required by law or as authorized by me. However, I understand that, from time to time, the coach may anonymously share general information for training or consulting purposes with other coaches.

ADMINISTRATIVE MATTERS:

Client will initiate calls if coaching is done by phone or SKYPE.

Payment will be monthly, in advance, by personal check, credit card or PAYPAL.

Sessions will generally be _____ minutes in length, starting at _____ and ending at _____ unless otherwise agreed to.

Coach requires _____ hours notice for cancellation of sessions that client cannot attend.

Cancellation will be by _____ (phone, text, email).

Failure to cancel results in _____

A reasonable number of emails between sessions are permitted as well as one phone call which must be kept to 5 minutes or less.

I agree to the above.

CLIENT SIGNATURE _____

DATE: _____

A Successful Coaching Outcome for Paul

Paul came to the coaching program uncertain about what coaching was. After our initial phone meeting, he quickly committed to the process. He kept all appointments or rescheduled with plenty of notice. He came to each session having completed the work assignments, which he generally sent in ahead of time.

We made significant progress in our second phone meeting by identifying a technical field career path. It was Paul's "aha" moment when he realized he could use his unique skills and competencies to truly launch his career. Once this was established, the job search became more focused and realistic. Paul was able to get multiple interviews and by the end of the three-month coaching engagement, he landed a position as a desktop support technician. Paul understood the skills he needed to continue to grow professionally and put together a good career plan. In Paul's responses to the follow-up survey, I was pleased to see that he felt the coaching helped him figure out what he wanted to do, helped him feel better about himself, and, equally important, made him feel supported. As a coach, you want the coaching experience to meet your client's goals, but you also want the client to experience the value that encouragement and support can provide.

Mary Kay Wedel (Certified Professional Coach) is president of Choice Leaders Consulting Group (Monmouth Beach, NJ) specializing in career management and executive coaching. She is also Senior Career Consultant at Lee Hecht Harrison (New York City) where she does career and transition coaching. Mary Kay received her bachelor's degree from Rutgers University and her coach training from iPEC (Institute for Professional Excellence in Coaching). She has served in leadership roles in the media industry for more than 25 years, with experience in marketing, communications, business development, and sales. Mary Kay lives in New Jersey.

PART II: MOVING FORWARD

CHAPTER 6

"BUT WHAT CAN I DO WITH MY LIFE?" NARROWING DOWN POTENTIAL CAREER CHOICES

By Deborah Tyson

> *"I have varied work experience in fields as diverse as finance, education, consulting, journalism, marketing, sales and government. The problem is that I am terrified of taking a job simply because I must and signing my soul away for the next 40 years."*
> —EZRA

> *"Identifying your lifework is no longer an escapist fantasy. It is a condition for being successful."*
> —WILLIAM BRIDGES, AUTHOR OF MANAGING TRANSITIONS

I come to this work with a passion for helping young grads "figure it out" in our ever-changing, complex world. I have the personal experience of going through it in my 20s, along with the strong and familiar feeling of angst it brings up—even more than a decade later.

I'm on the younger side of Generation X, so I walk the line between the generations. It gives me the advantage of getting where Millennials are coming from—even if it hasn't always been my direct lived experience. I have a distinct memory of my high school librarian telling me about this thing coming down the pike called the "world wide web," shortly before graduation; that about sums up my pre-internet era. I've coached many Millennials throughout my professional life in both a career coaching capacity and as a recruiter, a manager of volunteers, and a youth worker.

Here is what I know to be true:

1. Millennials want careers that are meaningful to them and that impact the world in some positive way. They value flexibility, leadership, mentoring, feedback, innovation, and balance. (Gallup, Inc. "How Millennials Want to Work and Live")

2. It is entirely possible and achievable for anyone to create a career that integrates much of what they want, enjoy, and are good at—it just takes some effort and courage. Finding this balance is especially important and relevant for the Millennial generation—because of the world they have grown up in, their shared core values and goals, and their place in the workforce.

3. Many twentysomethings have had terrible work experiences early in their career. They may blame themselves, the companies they worked for, their incompetent bosses, or the world for this bad fortune. Many grads have also lacked the support to make a strong transition from school to work. I see early career turmoil as a rite of passage and something that is required to give them the motivation to look for something different and more in line with who they are. If everything were perfect, without any thought or effort required, we wouldn't be having this conversation…and frankly, life would be pretty boring and predictable.

4. The world of work is changing, and Millennials are both leading this change and perfectly positioned to jump into it. According to a study by Gallup, Inc., "Millennials are altering

the very social fabric of America and the world. Defined by their lack of attachment to institutions and traditions, Millennials change jobs more often than other generations." Their lack of experience leads them to question and resist the status quo that many of us grew up with (e.g., one career for a lifetime, 9-5 jobs, and so on). Their tendencies and characteristics as a generation are, in fact, just what we need to move the world of work forward in new and innovative ways and solve many of our world's greatest challenges.

This next step in the coaching process is all about exploring options and analyzing the data collected in order to move the process forward. You've gathered the important information about what makes your client tick, and now is the time to make sense of it, play with it, experiment in the world, and make a hypothesis about a good professional path. (HINT: There are no wrong choices.)

> *"Don't ask what the world needs. Ask what makes you come alive, and go do it. Because what the world needs is people who have come alive." —Howard Thurman, educator and philosopher*

Using the College Major to Influence Career Direction
"How can my major actually translate into a job?"

This may be one of the first conversations you have with your clients. Many recent grads went to college without a clear career goal, especially if they studied something general, like liberal arts. The majority of students picked an area of study because it came easily to them or they found it interesting. Certain majors have always given students a lot of preparation for the workplace and some clear possibilities, while others require more creativity to align with careers.

The typical path for someone with a social science degree might be in the field of mental health, the nonprofit sector, or higher education. A student with a business degree might go into accounting, marketing, or management. Someone with a biology degree might become a researcher, go to graduate school, or move into health care. And there are, of course, a million other options, whether their major was easily translated for the workforce or not.

While it may logically seem that recent grads with a less directed major would struggle more to find their career path, that is not always the case. You may also come across grads who took a more traditional route and then found that they didn't want to pursue it, which leads to panicky statements like: "Yikes! What else can I do if this is the thing I have training in and I hate it?!"

Brainstorming Around a College Major

While some majors might not directly relate to a particular job, they can often jumpstart the brainstorming process and help grads to connect with what they are naturally interested in. In reviewing their major, suggest that Millennials include a look back at research projects they conducted, internships they held, and key contacts who could help them learn more about jobs in that field.

Often, majors provide less tactical guidance but translate more broadly into skills in critical thinking, problem-solving, and communication. The college major may have also sharpened your client's ability to learn new things and work in groups or a community. These are all valuable skill sets, the soft skills so prized in the workplace. If your client is not that connected to a major or can't imagine what he or she could do with it, do what coaches do best—facilitate a brainstorming session without judgment, uncover all the intangible skills and strengths your client does possess. It's often difficult to see these things for ourselves.

Ask grads to think of any and all things they did and learned about in college, paired with any dreams they've held or interests they have had, either spoken or never spoken out loud. Once they have gotten out all their ideas related to their school experience and put them down on paper, they can begin to map their skills and strengths to start to see what is possible, realistic, and appealing. I promise, those years in school were not useless—you may just need to help open your client's mind and get creative to come up with some new ideas about what is possible.

If a major makes the job discovery process easier for your client, great. If it makes it feel more stressful, let it go and begin to help open their mind to outside possibilities starting from a different direction. In addition to applying the skills gained in school (in academics as well as extracurricular activities), you can support your clients to pay attention to natural strengths, skill sets, and interests as they begin to narrow down their options.

The Grad School Fallback

Many grads lean towards graduate school as a backup to finding a job, if finding their place in the world of work feels too hard or confusing or they've had too many bad experiences. I may be old-fashioned, but I'm a firm believer that you should work for a bit before going back to school. By the time most students are 21, they have spent 15 or more years of their lives in a structured learning environment. Unless you choose to work in the educational field, the rest of the world does not operate that way. I advise clients to take time to explore the world and their interests and give themselves time and space to find clarity on their path before jumping back into school (especially if the choice is coming from fear, pressure from peers or family, or having no clue what to do).

I worked with a recent grad a few years ago who hadn't performed as well in college as she'd hoped and found herself in the field of marketing—with a few jobs that were a terrible fit for her. When I met her, her confidence had plummeted and she was 100% focused on getting into graduate school to explore other potential career options (such as nonprofit administration, creative writing, etc.). Her family had prestigious careers and were all highly educated. She wanted to meet their expectations of success, and graduate school was part of this definition. We worked together for six months and explored in detail her skill sets and core strengths, her interests and passions, and also simultaneously helped her to explore what worked for her—and what didn't—within her current role in a large corporation. She prioritized happiness over a traditional definition of success, but still felt stuck between "supposed to" and "want to."

During our work, she uncovered how important it was to her to use her creativity and to be a part of a supportive community that was doing good in the world. She landed a customer service position in a growing company that connects consumers with service providers, and she began to excel there. While she wasn't sure it was the place for her long term, it felt good to have some success and have a good experience professionally. The experience helped to build back her confidence, as did having the security of a paycheck.

Eventually she was able to move into a recruiter and HR role, which turned out to be the right fit for her. Had she jumped into grad school without first exploring her options and gaining some real world experience, it's likely she would have wasted time and money—and not have chosen a field that really suited her because her choice would have been based on an idea rather than a lived experience. Taking the time to experience a professional role is often one of the best ways to test the waters on whether or not it would be a good field for you for the long haul.

Brainstorm, Debrief, Explore, and Repeat

As a society, we are not typically trained to let our strengths and interests lead us. Millennials are much more comfortable with this than generations that came before them. However, they are being taught and mentored by other generations who were not raised this way. It's a breeding ground for misunderstanding. Traditionally, we were trained to be responsible and prioritize prudence. We were supposed to do the thing we were supposed to do and ignore our inner voice that was screaming NOOOOOO. Thankfully, Millennials are helping to change this dynamic.

The best way I've found to help my clients explore and narrow down options is simply to jump in. Do a brainstorming session with your clients by asking them questions like:

- Tell me about every job you've ever had (from fast food to camp counselor to full-time)
- What did you like about each of these experiences?
- Where did you excel?
- What did you want to run screaming from?
- What have you always imagined yourself doing for work?
- What did you want to be when you were a kid?
- What do your parents, friends, teachers want for you?

Once you have gotten all of these ideas and experiences out on paper, you can start to help your clients make sense of them. One of my favorite ways to do this is to have them create a list of their ideal job requirements and wishes–based on the information they collected about their college major and work experience. Once they have created the ideal, have them come up with a medium list that includes some concessions they'd be willing to accept. Finally, make the bare minimum list. Getting clear on what they think they might like to do is the first step.

Once your client has completed the full brainstorm and made some sense of the data collected, he or she can begin the exploring and narrowing process.

5 Ways for Grads to Narrow Down Choices and Find the Right Match

1. Align. See how your client's skills and strengths align with their dream job. There is a cool website called Jobscan.co (https://www.jobscan.co/) that helps applicants tailor their resume and cover letter to employers' job descriptions. But it can also be useful for clients who are searching for career direction. First, have grads search on LinkedIn or Indeed.com for a job description that really excites them, using a key word or job title. It can be aspirational. Side by side, copy and paste their resume and then the job description into the Jobscan program. Notice the overlaps and the gaps they may need to look at (not necessarily fix). Notice what skills and strengths emerge across the job description and resume. What resonates? Where could they enhance their skills? What skills do they possess that they simply forgot about? What is a marketing problem rather than a skills gap? This tool adds some realism to the mix by helping them see what hiring managers are looking for—but also helps grads view where their strengths shine and where they need further development.

2. Explore. Focus on companies they're interested in. Rather than endlessly searching for jobs online, search for companies that have a mission and culture that resonate. Millennials are highly skilled at internet research, and this is a great place to use that skill. Ask your clients to start with the company that interests them and then find ways to talk to people within those companies that could help them to find a good fit—based on their skills, strengths, background, and interests (e.g., via LinkedIn, Top Places to Work lists in their community).

3. Check for goodness of fit. Keeping focused on goodness of fit is one of the most challenging parts of a search for grads—especially when money is tight and rejection is unpleasant. Pull together the data they've collected during their self-assessment process. Make a spreadsheet of their skills, strengths, values, accomplishments, passions/interests, mission focus, etc. When looking at jobs that resonate with them, have them check for alignment of their values, skills, and strengths before applying blindly to anything that only sort of fits.

4. Consult the support team. Suggest they talk to the people who know them best. While a coach or mentor can be a great resource during a career transition, the people closest to them can also offer great insights. They can brainstorm with friends/family: What could you see me doing? What do you see as my greatest accomplishments? What are my greatest strengths? We all have blind spots for ourselves. The people who care about us and see the best in us can give important feedback.

5. Get real experience. There is nothing like real-world exposure to the field a grad would like to enter, based on the skills and strengths they currently possess. (This may be at a lower level than your client had hoped.) Volunteering or accepting a position at their current level will give them access to mentors and a chance to grow and learn about the organization and the field. Speculation about a given company or field will never completely match the real thing. No amount of internet research is ever a substitute for real experience.

Whether they end up enjoying the role or not, the data they collect is invaluable in finding the right fit for their career.

I recommend aiming high and being realistic about the time-frame for finding the right position. One of the common complaints about Millennials is that they want power and flexibility without having to work hard for it, as their parents and grandparents did. With a plan and some patience, they will get there. As their coach, you can help them to assess the data they are collecting and make educated choices about the best way to move forward.

Fear of Making the Wrong Choice

One of the most common things I hear with career changers, but especially with Millennials, is: "How will I know that I made the right choice?" and "What if I make the wrong choice?" My answer to fear and paralysis is always this: There is no wrong choice, just more data to plot along the way, giving you information for the future of your career. Multiple careers are the way of the future. You can't make a mistake here—it's all good learning. Whether the next job is amazing or could be better, you can't make it to the next step without engaging in the process and practicing. Crafting your professional life is a not a spectator sport; it requires grit, courage, and passion. Perfectionists may struggle to accept this, but I assert that this is a great place to begin the practice of letting go of "perfect."

Well-meaning family and friends may push grads to make the "smart" or "responsible" choice, to make a choice based on money—both in paying off loans, getting out of their parents' house, or to live at a certain lifestyle. Millennials are often struggling to compete, and they compare themselves with friends and siblings who are having more/less/different experiences than they are.

One of the unique qualities of this generation is that they are moving through all the traditional steps of growing up much later in life or not at all. Getting married, buying a house, having kids are becoming less "the thing to do." They have the freedom to take more risks, especially early in their careers. The hope is that the risks pay off down the road in greater satisfaction in their careers and lives.

And for my perfectionist clients: they may feel a lot of shame and guilt for not "killing this." Many have been very successful to date—they did well in school, got scholarships, were involved in extracurricular activities, had internships, won awards, and were seemingly well-prepared for the world! And then their first few jobs after school chewed them up and spit them out. As the wise Brené Brown once said, "Vulnerability is the birthplace of innovation, creativity, and change."

They Already Know What They Want

When clients come to me and say, "I have no idea what I want to do professionally," I listen lovingly to their words—but I just don't buy it. My experience has told me, and my deep belief in the coaching modality has shown me, that we always know deep down what is best for us. We just often need help uncovering it.

Millennials are part of a generation shaking up the status quo. The options are truly endless, which is often part of the trouble. Overwhelm can be paralyzing. Overwhelm without support often leads to swirling and inaction. Partnering with a trusted coach, advisor, or mentor who can help them explore their true interests and strengths, free of judgment, is often just what it takes for a recent grad to figure out this puzzle. It's amazing what the coach and grad uncover together. The answers truly are waiting for them. This answer won't come from a book, a blog, a video, or a person; it can only come from them.

Deborah Tyson (Professional Certified Coach) is a career and small business coach who received her training through iPEC (Institute for Professional Excellence in Coaching). Her professional experience includes 15 years working in the public and nonprofit sector within the fields of education, human resources, social services and nonprofit program management. She holds a Master of Arts in Intercultural Relations from Lesley University in Cambridge, MA. Debbie lives in Boston. To learn more about Debbie's coaching practice, visit her website at: www.mobilizecoaching.com.

CHAPTER 7

CREATE MOMENTUM! SETTING GOALS AND TAKING STEPS TO GET THERE

By Mira Simon

> *"Sadly, since graduation, I have lost my dreams. Currently, I am unemployed and spend countless hours a day worrying about what career path is best for my future. Despite months of soul searching I still am fairly clueless and realize that I need help to actuate a long-term plan."*
>
> —ROBIN

By this point in coaching, you have supported your young clients in understanding who they are, what motivates them and why, and have identified potential career choices that will reflect those choices. Now it's time to integrate all of that knowledge and awareness into helping them create a path for their vision to come to life. As we know, that's a lovely "coach-like" way to say that it is time to get into action!

This can be an exciting moment, as well as a time where overwhelm or stress may begin to set in for your client. And that is completely normal and totally okay. It's one thing for grads to take a deep dive into learning more about their passions, strengths, and values. Using those as a foundation to create their future path helps them feel less stuck, providing more excitement and motivation to move forward. It's another thing to then *move* forward.

As coaches, we know that it is not just about clients completing their "homework" or "action plan." At this point, it is also about whether they are implementing it and, if not, what may be getting in the way.

There could be external challenges, such as the need for better time management; or this could be the point when the internal roadblocks begin to surface. So it is important to support your client in recognizing when both external and internal challenges arise so they can address them. Here are a few of the internal thoughts that often come up.

"What will be different this time?"

Point out to the graduate that all of the work he or she has done up to this moment is what is different! This time they are using their values, passions, and strengths to identify their career choices, which will help them continue to navigate their journey. They will be able to use all they've accomplished thus far as their own individual GPS system—applying it to each action step they take to provide new input and information that will help them decide how they want to move forward and what they want to do for their next step.

"Where do I start?"

I don't know about you, but to me that is the hardest part. As a coach, when I work with my young clients, I will usually ask them a question like "How would you like to start?" or "What is one thing you can do to begin?"—knowing that the momentum of taking the first step energetically provides motivation.

As coaches, we also know that there is tremendous momentum in providing the client with information on exactly what to do, how to do it, and in what order, so that there is some basic process to follow. I love having a blueprint of where to begin that helps to know *how* and *where* to take that first step. I may not follow it exactly every time, but it definitely makes it much easier to begin. So fear not, that is what will be covered in this chapter.

"What if I get discouraged?"

As you know, in coaching there are often what appear to be steps backward just before there is tremendous growth. Additionally, there are no guarantees on how long it may take to find a job, and it's difficult to not get discouraged and/or take it personally. I just recently spoke with one of my former clients who was told she had gotten the job, pending background check, and had to wait over a month for that process. It's really difficult not to get discouraged when setbacks like that occur—both for the client AND the coach! As caring people, one of the first steps we can do to support our clients is to not "jump into the box" with them but to hold that space for them to express their frustration. Once they are able to do that, it clears the air of that energy and helps them to go more into creative thinking.

In the case of this particular client, we were able to challenge the thoughts and fears surrounding not receiving any feedback, having the client evaluate the validity of those fears by asking questions like, "How true is that scenario?" and "What might a different scenario be?" Then suggest they create a plan to translate the unknown void into getting information that will help them actually *know* what happened. You are helping them to access all they've learned and accomplished—how their individual GPS system is there to help them to course-correct based on their priorities, their path, and the outcome they want to achieve. And how to use that in *all* situations—in creating a plan, executing a plan on the job, and in life. It's like having your very own superpowers!

The 7-Step Career Plan

So, let's start! The 7-step plan below can be used to set the overall goals and action steps for a career plan, as well as the goals and action steps within the career plan. What's the difference?

Well, some people are more comfortable setting up their long-term career plan from a big-picture standpoint, like "I want to be CEO of a start-up company within the next 15 years." Others are happy to figure out the general pathway they want to follow and to create their next steps as they go. Their goal is to get out of thinking about what they feel they "should" do, and instead, tune into their own voice, and make choices from that perspective. Either way, this plan can be a great jumping-off place to set goals and action steps.

Most of the young clients I've worked with fit into the latter group, and having them set goals and plans based on their own authentic voice is a huge step forward.

The plan I use follows these 7 steps:

1. Begin with the end in mind.
2. Come up with the first step.
3. Build on the momentum of the first step to create your overall plan.
4. Set one specific goal to accomplish each day.
5. Design your follow-up system to keep track of your progress.
6. Continue to prioritize, reassess, and evaluate– based on values, goals, and events.
7. Lather, rinse, repeat—to accomplish the plan!

Below are the steps in more detail.

Step 1. Begin with the end in mind.

Using my favorite analogy of the GPS system, knowing the destination your clients want to reach helps them to figure out what the best path is to get there and helps them to make choices along the way to reach their destination.

As a coach, asking questions that create visions and ideal outcomes are a great way to begin while also coaching them to be as specific as possible when designing the outcome. As mentioned above, the "end" doesn't have to be 5 or 10 years down the road. It can be as close as "getting a job in my chosen field" or "figuring out what jobs are in my chosen career area." Momentum is created by accomplishing "mini-plans" that all add up to the overall goal (more on that in Step 4).

The more specific the outcome, the easier it is to design and accomplish the steps to get there, so specificity is a big part of this process.

One of my favorite stories comes from working with a recent college graduate named Stephanie who had just applied to medical school. She had been working at a doctor's office while waiting to hear back from schools and came to the realization that this life was NOT what she wanted. Although she and her parents had long intended that she would become a doctor, she saw that it was time to plan a career path that was based on choice rather than obligation. Together, we identified a few possible paths, and the initial outcome was "a career where there was flexibility." From that beginning, we got much more specific and came up with "what flexibility looked like to her" and "how she wanted to integrate that into the career path." Ultimately that helped us narrow down "what career path(s) would support her long-term."

The next step was to integrate all of the work she had done previously on identifying her strengths, skills, passions, and especially her values, in order to determine what career would incorporate all of them. Specifically, we looked at whether a career as a science teacher would be best suited to who she was, what she loved, and the specific outcome she had described—flexibility, time off, ability to work while having a family and be able to participate in their after-school activities, the opportunity for advancement if so desired, and not working in an office. Once she arrived at the career of teacher, you could visibly see the excitement and relief as a long-held vision was finally being realized! This opened the door to the next step, which is:

Step 2. Come up with the first step to start momentum.

The next question, after the client has come up with the overall outcome is "What is the *first* thing you want to do?" or "What is *one* thing you can do *today* to help you move forward?" That one thing may or may not be the logical first step, but it will get the client in action, and at that point you can come up with a list of steps to accomplish. This is extremely important because this is the actual "being in action." It involves all of the work that has previously been done—including visioning.

Using the example of Stephanie above, the first step that this client chose to do was to identify friends and family members who were teachers and find out more about the profession.

The first step for this grad could have easily been a number of different choices:

1. Look up different colleges in her area that offer teaching credentials.

2. Find out what the specific requirements are for a teaching credential.
3. Look up demand for teachers in the area.

What that first step is *does not matter* as much as the client choosing what he or she wants to do first and then executing it!

Step 3. Build on that momentum to create your overall plan.

I was working with another client, Doug, who realized that his first step was to stop looking for jobs online that he didn't want. His Step 3 was to open up a discussion with his family about what he really wanted to do. Energetically, that was a momentous step and was responsible for his ability to create his overall career plan.

Imagine, as a client, you've worked through all of the values and visions and energy around why you want to do it and what's kept you from moving forward. Now you're ready to create your plan, and you take the first step. Imagine the excitement of that moment. As coaches, that is one of the things we *live* for. Building on that momentum to create next steps is extremely important: it captures the excitement and celebratory energy and uses it to come up with the overall steps of the plan, which helps your client take a huge leap forward.

And that is exactly what Doug and I did. During that session, he mapped out his entire plan and the steps he would need to take to get there. We even came up with "parallel plans" that he could work on simultaneously as part of the overall outcome he wanted to create—a specific financial goal, along with the flexibility to work hours that would allow him to spend time with his baby daughter. One plan included using his strong networking skills to find a part-time job, as a way of creating an income stream. Another plan was specifically detailed as to what he needed to do to get an online business up and running. For each of the plans, there were specific due dates and timelines for when he wanted to complete each item.

Step 4. Set one specific goal to accomplish each day.

The importance of building on the momentum and staying in action cannot be emphasized enough. So a huge part of that is having your clients identify at least *one* thing they want to accomplish each day so that they stay in action and build on their progress.

Once we mapped out the next steps in Doug's plan, I asked him several questions:

1. What was the minimum he could accomplish each day?
2. What were potential roadblocks that might get in the way of accomplishing that task?
3. How did he want to be held accountable?

Doug suggested that he email me at the end of each day, letting me know he accomplished his goal—so that he also had a written record of his progress. I've also had clients text me, message me on Facebook, or even provide a brief call. It is important that both you and the client are comfortable with the plan and that you don't feel as if it is infringing on any boundaries for you. Many coaches I know include communication between sessions in the form of email or text, and this can be a fantastic way to keep your client in action and to forward the work that was done during sessions.

This system worked extremely well for him for several reasons:

- Setting up a minimum that he felt comfortable with helped him gain confidence early in the process, which helped him feel more excited and inspired to take action.

- It helped him to focus on what he did accomplish, rather than on what he wasn't doing. This was extremely important when he didn't hear back from potential employers or contacts right away. He could look at his emails and see when he had reached out and how much time had transpired, which, in many cases, was only a few days.
- Establishing an easily attainable daily goal helped him to go beyond that and feel like he was getting ahead much more quickly, which added to his confidence and momentum.

Step 5. Design your follow-up system to keep track of your progress.

The system my client Doug set up for accomplishing his goal and sharing his accountability worked well for keeping track of his progress, but what if your client chooses a phone call or some other less trackable method? Setting up a system, such as an Excel spreadsheet, to keep track of progress is essential so that there is a record of what was done, when it was accomplished, what the feedback was, and what the next steps will be.

One of my favorite conversations about looking for a job was the one I had with my nephew about how he approached his job search. This is a young adult who worked during high school and put himself through college working anywhere from one to three jobs at a time. In college, he had his eye on a particular restaurant job that was a coveted position because it was in a relatively small college town where there weren't a lot of opportunities to get jobs that paid well and could be done evenings and weekends. To say he had an organized, systemized approach would be an understatement. When I complimented him on it, he said, "Aunt Mira, looking for a job *is* a job—you have to put the same time, dedication, and work ethic into the process. If I work six hours *at* a job, then I need to spend six hours *looking* for a job."

BAM! Mic drop!

It took him two months, but needless to say, he got the job!

My nephew's follow-up system was not overly complicated. He marked down on his phone's "notes" app each time he called or stopped into the restaurant, noted what the response was, and formulated his next step based on the feedback he received each day. He designed the system that worked for him. As coaches, it is our role to guide our clients so that they are inspired to take this plan and create their own customized version, which they are excited to execute and motivated to accomplish. We can also ask for permission to suggest ways to do that. Ask your client about situations in the past, either with school or work, where they were responsible for keeping track of information:

- What was the information they needed to track?
- What was the system they used?
- How did they design it?
- What worked well?
- What would they change to enhance its effectiveness?
- How often did they update?

As illustrated in the example of my nephew, it doesn't have to be a formal Excel sheet—it can be anything that your client will be able to easily access, update daily, and provide a simple way to gauge progress.

For example, one of my clients went "old school" and kept a notebook of all of the companies she had reached out to. Each company had a separate page and she updated her progress daily, like a diary, so that she knew whom she had contacted, what the response was, and what her next steps were going to be.

Step 6. Continue to prioritize, reassess, and evaluate—based on values, goals, and events.

Now that there is momentum created and accountability established and a system in place, you can use the feedback and information to assess, evaluate, and prioritize. This is such an important step, and it is truly a huge opportunity for us, as coaches, to support our clients to use the events that happen as feedback for them to continually assess, evaluate, and choose how to interpret and integrate the events. To my mind, it is one of the major differences between consulting and coaching—where the client is able to experience what is happening to them, and through the coach's support, become empowered to use the experiences to move forward—in creating a career and in their life.

A very recent example is a client who had a specific plan for when he wanted to leave his job. Everything was moving along specifically according to plan, and he was accomplishing each and every step based on the timeline he had established. About a month before he was going to give notice, he showed up for our meeting, and I immediately knew something had shifted. The momentum was gone, the energy was gone, and he hadn't accomplished his weekly "assignment" as he had been doing all along. I asked him what was going on, and he told me that they had made an announcement that week about a huge quarterly bonus that was going to be given to the team. But the conditions were that it was going to be paid out at the end of two months, and in order for the entire team to receive it, everyone had to hit both their individual and team goals and be employed at the company.

This was a perfect time to evaluate his overall goals and plan, evaluate, and prioritize based on the values work he had done, as described in previous chapters.

We started by celebrating his accomplishments and success to date. I then asked him, "Let's say you woke up tomorrow and everything had worked out in the most ideal way, what would have happened?"

This gives clients an opportunity to share what they would love to have happen and for you, as a coach, to hear the value words that are part of that scenario.

He described that the ideal would be that he hit his individual goals a month early, was able to give notice at the beginning of the second month, so that he could still impact the success of the team and also be able to collect his share of the bonus. Then he would still mentally and emotionally feel like he was moving forward.

I asked him, based on his knowledge of the company and his direct reports, how confident he felt about that plan on a scale of 1-10 and he said a 2. He explained that while that would be the ideal, he felt that giving a month's notice might affect the overall momentum of the team and their ability to achieve the goal and that he didn't trust management to honor the month's notice.

My client's highest values were: trust, loyalty, freedom, flexibility, and family.

I then asked him, "In what ways are your values being represented here?" and "How can you use this to navigate this new information and create new steps moving forward?"

As a result of this reassessing process, he reprioritized, shifted his timeline, and moved his "give notice date" to a month later, safely after bonuses were secured. His feelings were that while the initial news felt like a huge obstacle in his path, in the scheme of his overall goals (and integrating his values of loyalty and flexibility), the loyalty to his team in the form of one more month far outweighed the ultimate freedom he would be creating for his future. He could totally be flexible for one extra month!

Step 7. Lather, rinse, and repeat—to accomplish the plan.

These steps are purposely created as a foundation for creating a plan throughout all stages of your client's career—whether it is for starting a career, continuing to build on one's current career, or even transitioning to a new career.

According to the Bureau of Labor Statistics, the average worker holds 10 different jobs before age 40, and the number of job changes is projected to grow. Forrester Research predicts that today's youngest workers, the Millennials and Generation Z, will hold 12 to 15 jobs in their lifetime and will be going through a job search every few years.

It is important to remind your clients that in every case, it is a marathon, not a sprint! Just as in running a marathon, you get to the finish line by accomplishing each step along the way, and each mile contributes to the overall goal. Each of the steps in the plan are milestones, and each needs to be celebrated and evaluated so that they can be efficiently and effectively used to get to the overall goal.

And, as any marathon runner will tell you, once you complete that race, it's on to choosing the next one—where it will be, when you will do it, and getting the motivation and inspiration that keeps you moving forward!

That's the beauty of having a plan.

Mira Simon (Certified Professional Coach) received her coach training from iPEC (Institute for Professional Excellence in Coaching), where she served as admissions coach. Prior to her coaching career, Mira spent over 25 years working in radio broadcasting sales and management. She graduated from the University of California, Los Angeles with a B.A. in Communication Studies. Her coaching company, Pathway to College, specializes in helping high school students discover their path and start making decisions that will propel their lives forward. To learn more about Mira's coaching practice, visit her website at www.coachmira.com. Mira lives in San Diego, CA.

CHAPTER 8

KEEPING DREAMS ALIVE WHILE MAKING A LIVING

By Madeline McNeely

> *"Why have I come to you? Because I want to build confidence around my choice to not pursue acting and find full-time work. I just want to work toward a profession that will make me enough money to support a family, a profession that will make a difference, and a profession that will make me happy. It has to be creative."*
> —KYRA

The first few years of a young person's career can set him or her up on a powerful professional pathway. The chance to do a variety of different kinds of assignments and projects early on gives recent graduates essential information about what they like and don't like to do.

Learning what our own innate strengths and gifts are in the first few years of work makes a big difference down the line. Developing a love of learning is a marker of someone who is more likely to be happy in their profession over the many decades of their work life. Curiosity, a desire to learn, and being comfortable with yourself when you start a new role and begin new tasks where you lack competence are essential qualities from which to build a successful career.

From my perspective in the leadership development field for almost 30 years and formally coaching for over 13 years, it's rare to know exactly what you want to do after college or to find work that leads directly to a lifelong career. However, early jobs can help us define career interests and skills and develop a vision. In my own case, I didn't know what I wanted to do after I graduated. I knew I cared about people and was interested in social issues. I followed in my sister's footsteps and took a job working in a group home for "emotionally disturbed" girls in Portland, Oregon. There wasn't anything more "disturbed" about these young women than me, except that they had far fewer resources to navigate the tragedies and pains of their childhoods.

Working with adolescent girls who were "wards of the court" taught me how much I cared about people's lives going well. This job showed me that doing what I loved and what brought me joy was one of the most important things I could figure out in life. I loved supporting someone with career issues, and I loved leading workshops and facilitating groups. This job also revealed to me how much of an interdisciplinary professional I was. It's not a coincidence that my career has taken the same interdisciplinary trajectory even at the age of 50, in my work as a coach, consultant, facilitator, trainer, and adjunct professor on a variety of leadership issues.

Most of us don't know what we want to do or who we want to be when we grow up, especially at age 22 when we officially enter the world of work if we're blessed enough to have spent four years after high school in college. I still wonder to this day about the professional choices I have made and the paths I didn't take. I am the kind of person who is interested in many different things, so I could likely have been happy in a variety of fields. A through-line of my career has been "do what you love and the money will follow." I have been willing and have had the privilege to ask myself over and over again what brings me joy and fulfillment even when the answer wasn't clear. When we name what we want to achieve and who we want to be professionally, it is much easier to draw this aspirational vision toward ourselves.

Kyra's Story: Taking Steps Toward a Long-Term Dream

A few years ago I was working with a young talented actor and filmmaker through the Grad Life Choices volunteer coaching program. Kyra had graduated from college a couple of years earlier as a film and theater major and was very excited to continue building her career as an actress and filmmaker. She made a number of difficult decisions before starting coaching. The main one was where to live post-college. She chose to move to Belgium and continue in the theater and film world as an intern, which she did for a few years. It was excellent experience, but she wasn't planning to live in Belgium forever. When she returned to the U.S., she decided to move back to her hometown of Pittsburgh. It was there that she realized she needed help to manifest her career aspirations. She was stuck, struggling to focus and feel like she could get where she wanted.

Because I have a background in the performing arts, Grad Life Choices matches me with creative Millennials—performers, actors, filmmakers, dancers, and so on. I was a modern dancer myself, so I know a lot about translating performance skills and experiences toward other professional tracks. Like the other coaches in the program, I am also an expert in supporting people in manifesting their dreams no matter what the field; so it is this combination that makes me a good coach for this group of Millennials.

I helped Kyra live into her long-term vision. She wanted to move to L.A. and continue her filmmaking career. When we started coaching, it had seemed impossible to her. But it wasn't. Through our work together, she eventually landed a job in L.A. working for a film producer and was thrilled with this outcome.

What made Kyra's story so successful? First, it was her drive to manifest her dream. She was aligned emotionally and mentally, as well as through her actions. She had a clear vision, but hadn't trusted herself to realize it. She needed support to break down her wishes into manageable, "chunk-able" steps she could implement. This was a focus of our work together. Professional coaches specialize in helping people "chunk down" their aspirations into baby steps so they can move ahead to realize their dreams.

The Interim Job: Paying the Bills While Growing Professionally

While Kyra was searching for a way to move into film, she had to pay her bills. When I started coaching her, she had found a job that wasn't exactly in her sweet spot, though it was somewhat related. She worked at a non-profit food kiosk serving foods from countries with which the U.S. was in conflict. This project was an educational venture funded by a university arts program and other foundations, and her co-workers were a very creative group of people. They produced art, did research projects, wrote as journalists, and educated themselves about the social issues affecting the countries whose foods were represented at the kiosk.

Kyra had chosen this temporary place of employment because it offered both community and an opportunity to make cultural and art connections. However, 90% of her work there was cooking and cleaning, which was discouraging. She explained how coaching helped: "I was able to see the parts of the job that catered to where I wanted to go next professionally, to be aware that I did have an opportunity to grow professionally there and to see where this job could take me." The creative atmosphere reminded her about what mattered to her, and for this reason it helped her to move forward in her career. She ended up working there for a year.

An outcome of this professional choice is that she completed three artistic projects, which took about 10% of her employed time at the restaurant, yet are still valuable to her today. She took a photography class through the university; she was able to build her portfolio; and she created her website. All were key steps in her professional journey. However, working in food service required a lot of mental energy on Kyra's part. She wasn't spending her time the way she wanted, so she had to keep finding ways to move toward her aspirational vision.

Practices to Move Toward a Vision

What were some of the steps we took together so Kyra could keep realizing her dreams?

1. Standards of success: This is an exercise I guide clients through to uncover and make visible their values personally and professionally. Examples of standards of success from clients include how much money they want to earn, office culture environment, commute time, work activities that are nourishing vs. draining. Whether you're 20 or 80, reviewing and declaring your "standards of success" grounds you in what really matters. We need to do this over and over again in our lives, because what matters to us when we're 22 is different than 35, 55, or 85, whether we're partnered, single, divorced, a parent or childless, and so on. This exercise was a rudder to help Kyra stay the course she was on.

2. Vision statement: Some of us have no problem articulating a vision for our lives and careers and some of us find this task daunting.

What is a vision statement? A short sentence or two that answers the question "What's different in the world and for you if you realize your mission?" Kyra did this assignment with relative ease. Her vision for the world was to "inspire people to come back to life with more vigor." To her this meant that she wanted people to taste life through art so that they would "wake up" thrilled and delighted with what's extraordinary about life. To get to this succinct statement, I asked her questions to draw out a variety of vision statements. We had to cull them down and work to make the final one simple, repeatable, and fulfilling the "juice factor." Did it make her excited to say? Could she remember it? The answers were yes, and we succeeded in completing this element of our work.

3. Mission: A professional mission statement is about your calling or vocation in the world. What are you being called to do? Kyra's mission statement is *storytelling through the camera*. More specifically she directs video content: commercial, documentaries, and PSAs using cameras to tell stories in short form. This is what she is called to do daily in her career. My professional mission statement is also my company's mission statement: *to condition leaders and organizations to do meaningful work for decades*. A mission statement might also be a tag line. It's part of your professional brand. It is used as a compass to gauge if you're heading in the direction you think you want to go.

4. Strengths inventory: There are formal and informal ways to do this, but essentially it's important to match our perceived strengths with what others perceive as our strengths. Kyra was asked to interview at least five people in her life professionally and personally to help her align her self-perception with how others saw her. Throughout our careers we will move toward our next aspirations with greater ease if we're in alignment about what our strengths are and are not.

5. Skills: Another part of our work to ensure that Kyra landed where she wanted to was identifying succinctly what she knew how to do. Skills are both tactical/practical and emotional/mental in nature, both the soft and the technical elements. Kyra had many skills as an actor, photographer, videographer, organizer, and producer. We created a list that she could easily share with prospective employers and talk about confidently.

6. Components of your ideal job: What is the ideal work environment, and what do you want to be doing and learning? Millennials want to learn and grow. We all want this as humans, but Millennials are pushing leaders to take this more seriously and integrate it more often in the workplace. The world moves at a much quicker pace, distances are shrinking due to technology. Kyra knew that the clearer she was with herself and prospective employers about her skills and goals, the easier it would be for her to find a good professional match. She wanted to be in L.A. as an artist, but she also knew that if she could find work in a virtual workplace she would work anywhere, as long as she was learning and growing her craft. When she listed her ideal work environment and tasks, she was able to discern quickly whether a potential job was the right fit for her. She could prioritize what really mattered to her.

7. Networking: Many people find networking to be quite intimidating. Millennials often feel as if they don't have anything to offer someone with whom they want to network. In Kyra's case, she found people who were only a year or two ahead of her professionally rather than contacting people who were much older and further along. She called this "peer networking." Once she found those professionals whom she could emulate, she had a model for how to maneuver through her immediate challenges. She could see in reality where she wanted to be and what she had to offer, and this gave her hope and drive to keep moving toward her dreams. In return, she offered to help them for free on their creative projects. The social aspect of networking proved critically important for Kyra. Part of her weekly homework assignments was to email and call people whom she admired professionally. This pushed her outside her comfort zone and built her confidence muscles so she could step toward her aspirations with greater ease and self-assurance.

8. Personal branding: This is an aspect of career development about which artists know a lot. Performers are constantly "selling" themselves to get the next opportunity. It's essential for artists to have websites, videos, headshots, etc., about who they are and their craft. This confidence at selling oneself is a critical skill to ensure one can reach long-term aspirations. We must be comfortable with this part of career development because it requires lifelong attention to do well. Kyra spent the first few sessions working with me on finishing her website. What seems like an impossible task to this technology Luddite leadership coach, she was able to gestate and birth in weeks. Knowing and confidently putting one's personal brand out into the world is a big distinguishing factor between those who succeed and get where they want to go and those who flounder.

9. Embodying your vision: The most important element that Kyra and I worked on was training her repeatedly to embody her vision and take a stand for her aspirations as she took steps toward her vision. She learned a four-part centering practice called Leadership Embodiment to help her do this well, based in the work of Wendy Palmer (http://www.embodimentinternational.com/). She did the practice regularly, which helped her embody her vision and ultimately land where she wanted to be. As Kyra explained, "Practicing the breathing and postural exercises instilled confidence, which was reflected in my physical presence. I carried that into interviews and talking to peers about what I wanted to do. I learned not to shrink my body or to be afraid to talk about myself."

Kyra's life in L.A. is going as she has designed. As of this writing, she is freelancing about seven 12-hour days a month, writing treatments for other directors and producers, and producing a commercial. The rest of the time she works on her own short film projects, which she creates on spec in hopes that production companies will pick them up.

Coaching Lessons That Last

While I was writing this chapter, I reached out to Kyra as she was beginning her new job in L.A. Kyra said the following lessons from our work together had proven crucial:

1. Keep looking at the baby steps to get closer to your dreams.
2. Find people who are in communities you want to be part of.
3. Do weekly assignments to stay on track. Kyra said our coaching offered accountability and a sense of time and scheduling. Since she was living with her parents during our coaching, Kyra had to focus extra diligently on herself and her vision, in part because her mother wanted to do mother/daughter activities and escape her own professional challenges. Kyra enjoyed these, but it was hard for her to stay focused on her own development. Coaching was a reality check for her. She learned to ask herself, "A week has passed. Have you noticed? What have you accomplished?"
4. Have compassion for yourself. Kyra was initially self-critical that she couldn't accomplish this work on her own. She

realized that "we all need support to get where we want to be in life."

5. Journaling and writing down your thoughts can help you stay motivated.

6. Words matter. She realized that her conscious thoughts and the words she used about herself could help or hinder her success.

7. Making money from commercial interests doesn't take away from professional integrity. The coaching work we did together helped her get over some of her "holier than thou" mentality around money and freed her to develop the skills and do work she enjoys, while being practical about her need for income.

8. Don't be afraid to negotiate for salary. Kyra appreciated that I made myself available during the negotiation stage of landing her job in L.A. Supporting Millennials in negotiating, particularly women, is a game changer in their careers. The sooner we learn to do this, the better financial outcomes women will have over the course of their lifetimes.

The learning process that Kyra and I, as her coach, went through never ends. She's looking for richer experiences in her life as a result of the work we did together. She has a deeper template for what's possible in her career. And she's continuing to shoot for the moon while growing professionally and personally.

Madeline McNeely's mission is to condition leaders and organizations to do meaningful work for decades. Madeline is a multi-sector, interdisciplinary professional serving in the roles as executive leadership and career coach, consultant, facilitator, trainer. She teaches *Leadership Coaching Strategies* and *Non-Profit Leadership and Community Engagement* at Harvard Extension School. Madeline is passionate about the performing arts and social justice education. She is certified in Conversational Intelligence (C-IQ), Leadership Embodiment and Integral Yoga. She has a B.A. in Development Studies from Lewis & Clark College and an M. Ed from Temple University. Madeline lives in the Boston area. Visit www. conditioningleaders.com

CHAPTER 9

GRAD SCHOOL OR NOT?

By Sue Hall

"I have thought about pursuing a second bachelor's degree as well as graduate school to get a more applicable degree, but it seems like everyone I ask tells me something completely different."
— *LINDSAY*

It is common for graduates to consider whether an advanced degree is right for them. They may be seeking career opportunities after achieving their undergraduate degree and may discover they lack the education or credentials for the career that they would like to pursue. But they also want to be sure that taking on additional debt is a practical and productive choice.

There are many things to consider in making this decision, with potentially long-lasting impacts on career options, advancement, and financial commitments. Not every career benefits in the same way from an advanced degree, and the timing of the achievement can make a difference as well.

This chapter will help you guide the young person you are coaching through the decision-making process, taking into account the why, when, how, and where of making this choice.

Exploring the 'Why'

Motivation: What is the real motivation behind your client's pursuit of an advanced degree? It may be required or it may be to increase their earnings. It may be to become more competitive in a field, especially if the university they hope to attend is highly rated. It may be for the pure love of their field of study and the desire to learn more. Or it may be because they don't know what else to do and think grad school will help them decide. Some deeper questions to consider: Is it because they truly want an advanced degree or because they think they should? Is it because everyone else is doing it? Is it because they are avoiding getting a "real" job and becoming an adult (they enjoy being a student), or because the job market is so tough they are reluctant to face it? Or does getting an advanced degree help fulfill some need to be the "best" (perfectionism), to be enough? Exploring all this with your Millennial clients will help them understand why they are pursuing graduate school and whether it is in alignment with their values and goals.

How important is an advanced degree in their field? Encourage your clients to research their career choice to determine what it takes to be hired in their industry. You might ask them how they can gather information from various resources. For instance, they could speak to company or organization recruiters even if they aren't applying for a current job posting—most will be happy to give advice.

- Questions grads may consider asking a recruiter: What are hiring leaders looking for? Regardless of the requirements for the job, what is the education level of the people they typically hire?
- Questions they may want to ask themselves: If they get an advanced degree, are they pricing themselves out of the

market? If most hires in their chosen industry typically don't have an advanced degree, and they do, will they expect to earn more? Will the market in that industry support that? Some fields require an advanced degree to be hirable, but for some it is more a perception than a reality. And in rare cases an advanced degree could be a disadvantage.

What are their long-term goals? Encourage young clients to think about what they might like to do further in the future in their career. Are they interested in leadership (e.g., becoming a business leader, for which they might need an MBA)? Do they see themselves as practitioners or academics—as teachers or as researchers? Many graduates who go down the path of academia find that an advanced degree is necessary to become published and tenured. What credibility do they gain from their advanced degree and exactly what does it allow them to do? Are there additional gains in responsibility that are tangible?

Will they enjoy it? Since they will be taking mostly classes in their chosen field, they should really look forward this part. If they don't, they might wonder about their career choice, and you can help them determine if it really represents their life goals.

Same or different field? I have worked with many adults who are doing something other than what they majored in, myself included. I worked with a graduate who went all the way through law school—and then decided he didn't want to be an attorney. But he had invested too much time and money in obtaining his degree to simply abandon it. We did a lot of brainstorming about what he could do instead, and what might exist within his field that he hadn't thought of. He ended up seeking a role as an attorney with an animal rights activist group.

Have they done research? My advice to all college grads is to spend significant time on the internet researching their field. They can find sample interview questions for most common fields online, which might help them decide if they are truly interested in that field. I also encourage searching under "unusual careers" plus their chosen field online. There are many job opportunities that they may not have thought of. For example, as the department leader of a training team inside a large financial services institution, I've hired a lot of former teachers. I think most people going into the education field think about teaching elementary through high school and don't think about an adult business audience.

My stepdaughter is a great example of using grad school to change fields. When she started college, she wanted to be a magazine writer or novelist, so she majored in English. However, she felt she probably wouldn't make a living in that field very easily, so she changed her major to education. She did very well in her teaching practicum but hated it. After graduation, she landed a job in a nonprofit inner-city daycare center and loved it, but wanted to rise higher. She went back for her master's degree in nonprofit management—a completely different field from where she started!

A young woman I coached in the Grad Life Choices program had a degree in fine arts. Allie had sent me examples of her work, and it was clear she was extremely talented. A dream job for her would have been curator of an art museum or being able to sell her own art through galleries. However, she knew that the odds of either one of these things happening was low, especially as a young artist. Allie also had a strong talent in computer science and made the decision to go back for an advanced degree in this area. In researching the requirements, she found that she had to take some undergraduate-level math classes in order to get into the master's program. Fortunately, she was able to test out of several other basic classes. Allie ended up applying for the master's program twice, and on the second try she got in! She was able to come to terms with the idea that the money she would make in her computer science role would help pay for opportunities to further her passion for fine arts. We also had several coaching sessions to build the connection between the creativity of fine arts and the creativity of computer science.

Certification—another alternative: Millennials should look into whether they could qualify for their chosen career by getting a professional certification rather than an advanced degree. Certifications are shorter-term, less expensive, and frequently offered online. They should make sure, however, that certifications are readily accepted in their field. They can always continue with an advanced degree post-certification if they decide later that they want to pursue an additional credential.

Exploring the 'When'

Timing: How will your young client take into account career and personal timing? Coaches may wish to prompt grads to think about what might be the best time in their life to pursue an advanced degree. What is their personal situation at this moment? What do they predict in the next few years? There is some logic to getting an advanced degree sooner rather than later, based on their plans regarding relationships and having children.

Do they want to take a year off first? Many graduates are tired of being in school. They may think, "I'll have a break, then I'll go back for my advanced degree." Coaches could ask questions related to the reality of going back after a year away and other factors they may wish to take into account.

Can I get my advanced degree later? Explore the likelihood of whether or not they can get started in their career without an advanced degree and achieve it later. Is it possible to begin their career now, build their resume, pay off some debt, and learn more about their field first? Have they thought about where they want to work? Big firm or small firm or starting their own company? Many large, established companies offer tuition reimbursement, a great benefit not found elsewhere. Be sure they understand the company's requirements for repayment. If they leave within a certain time, they may need to pay it back in full!

The impact of relationships: I worked with a young woman who was a top student during her undergraduate years and then found herself working full-time and in a serious relationship. The man was older than she and wanted them to be married and start a family as soon as possible. She was very torn about the timing of her goal to get an advanced degree. Through coaching, she determined to do journaling and create a vision board to help her decide what she wanted. These activities helped her connect with her vision and passion, as well as what she liked to do for fun (journaling). Ultimately, she came to the conclusion that her personal differences with her boyfriend were holding her back in a way that made her uncomfortable, and she ended the relationship.

Exploring the 'How'

Staying with the same field or changing fields: Does an advanced degree support the client's current undergraduate degree, or will it lead to a different career choice? I have worked with students who are pursuing an advanced degree that is in alignment with their undergraduate degree. In this case, it is easier to enter the program at the correct level. If they are pursuing an advanced degree in a completely different field from their college major, they should find out what they need from a placement standpoint—are there classes they need as prerequisites and can they test out of any of them? It could delay their entrance into an advanced program.

Funding: Scholarships, loans—ask your clients questions about how they are going to pay for their program. They are likely to have debt from their previous undergraduate education. Understand how their loan works and when repayment begins, whether or not they stay in school for an advanced degree. Will their current loan repayment be deferred if they stay in school? What loan options exist for advanced degrees? Based on their undergraduate performance, do they qualify for any scholarship opportunities? I have worked with grad students who qualify for scholarships based on economic status or ethnicity. Also, what opportunities exist to have a work/study program at the university? This program can advance their education through mentoring as well, since they might have the opportunity to work directly with one of the professors in their major field of study. They might also gain new experiences, such as grading papers or possibly even delivering a class lecture or teaching a section.

Encourage your Millennial to think about what student loan repayment will feel like and how it fits with the rest of their lifestyle. They should think about their place of residence and their car or other transportation they will need. What is the longevity of those current situations? Think about potential upcoming significant expenses. I've worked with students with medical needs, and everything should to be taken into account. Millennials might not see around the corners quite as well as someone with our experience!

I worked with a young woman who was not close with her father. Even though he was wealthy, she was determined that she would never ask him for money. After several coaching sessions in which we explored this topic, she felt that asking for funding for graduate school was very different than asking for money for general living expenses. She did ask him, and he agreed to help her! She felt proud of the courage she summoned to take this step—and was grateful to her dad for his help, opening the door to a renewed relationship.

113

Do the math: What difference in the long run will this decision make regarding the client's opportunities and financial situation? Encourage them to do their own personal math. Based on the cost of the program they want to attend and the resulting debt including the interest charged on their loans, compared to their projected income and other expenses—does it add up in the positive column?

Application: The application process can be quite extensive. At the very least, your clients will usually need to take an exam, such as the GRE (more about this below), submit their undergraduate transcript, and write an essay and a personal value statement. They can find examples online, and you can help them shape the message it contains. It is important that it contains facts and specific examples, but also speaks to their passion for their future degree and career choice. How will they make a difference in the world with this advanced degree? There is stiff competition, and universities are usually looking for the best. Writing this type of essay requires them to shift their mindset from that of a student to that of a professional making a contribution in the real world.

References: When applying for an advanced degree, they will typically need at least three references. It is important to have references from professors in undergraduate college who valued their performance in class. They might also ask you for a reference letter. I have written several references for grads based upon their dedication to coaching. You can help them determine who they want to ask for a reference letter and ensure that these are completed within any stated deadlines. All references are submitted online directly from the person giving the referral to ensure security.

Exploring the 'Where'
Location: Help them to understand what options they have regarding the location of the university. What already exists in their

community? Do they want to relocate, and can they afford to? Ask how they might be able to research a new city and its opportunities for post-graduate education as well as housing, etc. What benefits might they gain from going to an online university?

Same or different university: There are multiple schools of thought on this issue. Encourage them to explore whether or not they should stay with the same university where they received their undergraduate degree. This choice may differ based on their field of study and/or their university. Some universities prefer an undergraduate and post-graduate degree from different universities, as it may help the student be more well-rounded and increase their exposure to different schools of thought.

Some students will select a university in the state where they want to ultimately work. Certain degrees that require licensure are best completed in the state where they will practice, since that program may focus on the specific requirements of the state.

Accreditation: Determine if companies or entities in your field tend to hire more frequently from a certain university or type of university. Inquire if there are schools that have specific accreditations that are either well received by hiring leaders or perhaps required. Most important, be sure that the school is currently accredited. Some for-profit institutions have lost their accreditation, making their degree worth much less and losing the ability to participate in government loan programs.

Internships: Have the young person explore whether the university places its graduate students in internships or whether they will need to seek out their own placements. For example, my daughter is completing her undergraduate degree in psychology. She discovered that the university she wants to attend for graduate school has a wonderful placement record for local internships and practicums due to its proximity to multiple special needs organizations.

Entrance tests: Some universities require the GRE exam to be completed with a certain score or above for entrance, while others do not. Students should allow time to prepare and take the test multiple times if necessary. They can purchase new or used study materials, including a book and on-line version.

State-to-state differences: Does an advanced degree allow the students any additional licensure in their field? What happens if they move to another state? Frequently, state licensure exams differ. Many do not transfer from state to state, and if young people move after graduation or in the future, they may need to retest to obtain a license to work in their field.

Exercises That Help with Decision-Making

Here are several exercises that a coach might suggest to Millennials to help them determine their decision about obtaining an advanced degree or to clarify their thinking. They can do this for homework and go over it at the next coaching session or on their own. Some of these exercises require inner work that is beneficial at any stage of life.

Vision board: By placing items that are meaningful to you on a vision board, you can create a visual montage that inspires and clarifies your thinking. You can do this manually placing items on a posterboard or digitally with free apps like the Hay House Vision Board. Your young clients would go through a process to clip and save things that appeal to them, both professionally and personally. Once completed, ask them to take a step back to study what they have created, what do they see? Is there alignment personally and professionally—with values, future choices, where they want to live and how? A vision board can be changed and added to as time goes on.

Keeping a journal: Some young people benefit from journaling their thoughts and ideas and allowing time to pass. As they reflect back on their thoughts later, they may have some self-discovery moments that help them make decisions about their life and career.

Role play: You might offer to role play with them, which can help in a variety of circumstances. Many people whom I coach speak about the benefits of sharing something out loud with another person rather than just thinking about it. Once they hear themselves say it, it seems to sometimes resonate differently. They can see what fits them and what does not.

Portfolio/work samples: When I'm coaching at a distance, I have asked Millennials to send me samples of their work (typically a photo or writing via email, or a link to their portfolio, if they have one). I ask questions about how they plan to market themselves and their work in order to be accepted to an advanced program at the university to which they're applying.

Job shadowing: Before they choose to go for an advanced degree, encourage your clients to gain an understanding of a "day in the life" of a professional in that role. Some companies and organizations will allow opportunities to job shadow, even if you are not interviewing. It is also a wonderful opportunity for job seekers to make themselves visible to a company or organization in which they may want a future internship or career. Many industries are very open to having a young person job shadow. My son changed his mind about what he thought his career would be after a job-shadowing experience. He had thought he wanted to be a physical therapist for children. He visited this exact setting, and it just wasn't what he had envisioned. Ask grads how they can find out what pre-application experiences are available.

Informational interview: Similar to a job shadowing, the informational interview offers the opportunity to practice interviewing in a low-pressure environment. One question to ask is whether this company or organization hires advanced degree recipients from any particular universities with greater regularity. Informational interviews with a representative of the graduate school program itself are also useful. I worked with one post-graduate who found out that his prospective grad school was seeking diverse students and had set up an "exploration" meeting for applicants with professors to find out more about what the university offered. This presented an excellent opportunity for networking and becoming better informed about the program's goals and content.

Putting It All Together

Deciding whether to go for an advanced degree is an extremely important decision. A post-graduate degree can help you launch the career you have long desired; or, conversely, it can absorb a great deal of time, putting you deeply in debt, without much if any gain. So, before taking this significant step, young people need to think hard about why they are doing it, whether it really meets their needs, how they can manage the financial and time requirements, and where it makes most sense to pursue their degree. With the help of a coach, the grad can explore each of these subjects through responses to probing questions and a variety of helpful exercises. They could find the experience invaluable!

Sue Hall (Certified Professional Coach) currently works as senior business coach for Edward Jones, one of the largest investment firms in the United States. Sue has more than 30 years of experience as a financial professional. Her role at Edward Jones is to coach new financial advisors all across the country from start to 36 months, and to coach veteran staff on request. Sue is also a licensed financial advisor and is a member of her team's committee for Associate and Leadership Development. She received her coach training at Coach University. Sue is based in St. Louis, MO.

CHAPTER 10

GETTING EXPERIENCE WHEN YOU HAVE NONE

By Elise Oranges

> *"Lacking experience right out of college is tough because potential employers feel like they may be taking a risk on someone with a greater learning curve."*
> —NATE

The path to finding a job and growing a career today differs greatly from when many of us graduated from college. Back then, you went to school, got a degree—and then you could be pretty sure that you'd get a beginning job where you would gain some experience and decide if that was what you really wanted to do. Many companies had training programs for new grads, and entry-level jobs were plentiful.

The job path for college grads today is quite different. Due to the changing economy—and the increase in such factors as global competition, technology, robotics, and outsourcing—full-time permanent jobs are in short supply. American workers with experience who lost their jobs during the recession are willing to accept entry-level positions at lower salaries. This has led employers to expect new hires to have experience—not only in the technical aspects of their chosen field, but also in general business operations and "soft skills," such as effective communication, positive attitude, and team-work skills.

Today, a diploma and college education are no longer enough by themselves to guarantee landing a good job. Now you need experience just to get an entry-level job! But how can you get experience when you don't have a job? And how can you get a job when you don't have the experience? This seems like an insurmountable "Catch-22" for many grads.

Good news! There are alternative ways for recent grads to get experience while looking for the elusive full-time job. These non-traditional avenues include:

- Internships
- Volunteering
- Freelancing
- Part-Time and Temp Work
- Entrepreneurship

The tough part is that these require taking responsibility for one's own career and creating one's own path. This may not be what college grads want to hear, because they may be holding onto some of those outdated beliefs. But the reality is that we can't rely on anyone or anything to get us where we want to go. Nor can we just sit around waiting for something to happen. Doing something, almost anything, is better than doing nothing, in both job hunting and in life!

Benefits of the In-Between Time

Internships, volunteering, freelancing, part-time and temp work, and entrepreneurship can provide graduates with education, experience, insight, and connections that can lead not only to a job, but to something that they're really excited about! Here are some of the benefits:

- Grads can "try out" a job, industry, or prospective career path to determine if it is right for them—before committing an enormous amount of time and energy to the field. It's better to find this out now, rather than spend years in an unsatisfying job or profession and then have to figure out what to do next.
- They can build real-world skills and experiences that enhance their resumes, demonstrating productivity and a great work ethic to potential employers.
- They can obtain networking opportunities: getting to know people in the industry, asking questions and learning from them, and building relationships.
- Employers get to "try out" potential employees see if they'll fit into the organization's culture and if they have or are capable of developing the skills the company or organization is looking for.

Whether your young clients are having a hard time finding the career they were hoping for, are realizing that job security is a thing of the past, or are feeling constrained by working for others—these opportunities allow them to gain work experience while they're searching for that perfect full-time job or career. There is much to be learned and many valuable skills to be gained by creating different streams of income/experience or starting up and running their own business, however small it might be. And doing productive work keeps their spirits up and their minds sharp.

Some of the grads I've coached have used one or a combination of these alternatives to full-time employment to either gain more experience to qualify for a full-time job, explore new fields, or start their own business.

For example, one client, Zoey, who had earned a bachelor's degree in journalism and a master's in adult education, couldn't find a job in either field. She was working part-time demonstrating beauty products for a home shopping channel while also developing instructional programs for corporations and organizations. She wanted a coach to help her figure out an appropriate career path to make use of her education, talents, and her interests in high-end fashion, beauty, and lifestyle products. In our early sessions, we discovered that there wasn't one specific type of job that appealed to her and fit her talents and interests. When I suggested the possibility of having several part-time jobs in different fields in order to get experience, try out each of them, and possibly create her own consulting business, her response was, "Oh, thank goodness, I thought you were going to tell me I had to get a real job!" Together we mapped out a path for her to get where she wants to be in the future.

Another grad, Leo, had a B.A. in English and religious studies. He had held a brief editorial internship at a start-up publishing network, had worked for a local office of a minor political party doing canvassing and fundraising, and had been published in various publications since he was in high school. When we met, he was walking dogs to pay the bills and doing freelance writing for a political news and opinion blog. He needed help finding the right career, something related to his skills that was also meaningful. Sometimes he thought he wanted a full-time job that would allow him to make enough money to support himself and get a place of his own. Other times he was more focused on writing about meaningful topics. We spent some time looking at entry-level jobs in publishing and library work, but he wasn't very enthusiastic about them. He had an enterprising spirit and wanted to make an impact quickly. Meanwhile, he started up a new blog for writers. With more published writing credits under his belt and a growing list of professional references, he was well positioned a few months later to be hired for a job he was really excited about—as a breaking news reporter for a major publication in the Northeast.

Jack had a B.A. in communications with an emphasis on organizational communication. He wanted to work in human resources. His experience since graduating from college was mostly in education, as a substitute teacher, and when we met he was working part-time as a bartender. He wasn't quite sure which specific area of human resources he wanted to be in, and those jobs that he was interested in required—you guessed it—experience! He was interested in interpersonal relationships, so together we designed a plan for him to start a Meetup group to teach guys how to talk to girls. I understand that he has since started working for a magazine that celebrates "a mix of adventure, expertise, and kindness," a good combination for his multiple talents and interests.

How can alternative work situations such as these benefit your Millennial client? The following is an overview of each.

Internships

An internship is a fixed-term work assignment with a company or organization that usually involves specific tasks or projects as well as assisting in other special projects, presentations, and undertakings. Some see internships as temp jobs without the pay, but internships can be a valuable tool for learning and gaining experience. They also have the potential to lead to a permanent, full-time position with the company at the end of the assignment, as some companies use internships as a recruitment tool.

Companies and organizations want to hire employees who already have professional experience under their belts. Internships provide opportunities to network, learn job skills, and gain a better knowledge of the workings and day-to-day tasks of a chosen profession. In addition, the fixed duration of the internship gives the intern extra time to consider his or her career choices in a real-world setting. Since the majority of internships are offered to college undergraduates, often in exchange for college credit, this option might not be available after graduation. Still, it's worth looking into internships on job boards to see if recent grads are eligible; in that case, such positions are likely to be paid.

Volunteering

Volunteering is a valuable tool that provides real rewards and benefits. It's the first thing I recommend to all of my career coaching clients, whether they're just getting started in their careers, getting back into the workforce, or considering changing careers. It's another way to "try out" a new career or field of interest, learn more skills, meet people, and help others at the same time. But for Millennials especially, who place high value on purpose and work–life balance, volunteering allows them to not only learn and gain experience, but also to look outside themselves and help a cause that they're passionate about.

There are likely very few places that will turn down offers for free help, so volunteering provides a wide variety of opportunities to not only learn how organizations work but also to develop one's own self-confidence and the ability to work with others. Volunteer experience could also even spur one to think about a different career path.

The drawback to volunteering is that it's unpaid, so care must be taken when determining how much time the grad is devoting to volunteering and how it fits into his or her specific financial situation.

Freelancing, Part-Time, and Temp Work

While volunteering is a great way to get skills to put on a resume and develop contacts, it also helps to have some paid gigs. Most grads can't afford to only volunteer. Freelancing, independent contracting, and part-time or temp work all help to build up a portfolio that can be presented to future employers. Part-time and temp work afford "tastes" of one or several different positions or industries while still allowing time to research full-time positions or pursue other interests. Both also have the potential to lead to full-time jobs. Temping and part-time work tend to be office jobs. These can often be found through staffing agencies in different fields. Sometimes these jobs are advertised as "temp to perm"—in which case a one-to-three month stint has the potential of turning into a full-time staff position.

Freelance or contract work has traditionally been common in media, journalism, public relations, design, writing, and computers and information technology. Nowadays, however, it's becoming common in almost all areas as a result of technology, and more and more companies and organizations are outsourcing more and more of their work. This allows businesses to remain lean and flexible, and, of course, save money.

On the positive side for grads, freelancing or contract work allows them to make money and build experience quickly, whereas permanent positions can take many months to secure. Working under contract on a creative project can be more interesting than routine office work. Often such jobs can be done offsite, with occasional scheduled meetings. As long as the project comes in on time, the contractor is typically free to work his or her own hours, and work for other employers as well. The downside is that employers will not be responsible for paying employment taxes or health benefits for independent contractors. Grads must be sure to pay taxes and social security on their own. Nor will they receive vacation pay, training, or other benefits. In addition, they will have to re-market themselves to a new employer at the end of every contract job.

Freelancing as an independent contractor has the potential to lead to steady part-time work and/or a full-time position. Working as a freelancer can also lead one to see possibilities that might not have been apparent before, paving the way to a new career path or business idea.

Entrepreneurship

An entrepreneur is a person who conceives of, organizes, and operates one or more businesses. Typically, an entrepreneur starts out small and offers a product, process, or service for sale. Sure, there are businesses that require a lot of capital to get started, for things like office space, heavy equipment, or staff. These require financial investment, risk, and a long-term commitment to building your own business. That's beyond the scope of this chapter. Here we will focus on small business start-ups, or side businesses, that are usually based on service or knowledge (see "Freelancing" above). These also happen to overlap with many fields that offer entry-level jobs, so the experience is transferable.

Starting a small business can help a college grad to develop organizational, marketing, sales, and other "soft skills," such as communication and teamwork. It shows a potential employer that this applicant is accountable for his or her own actions, is aggressive, knows how to execute, is adaptable to change, and has the innovative, positive goal-oriented attitude that is necessary to be successful in business today. Whatever talents grads put to use, whether designing websites, marketing homemade products on Etsy, or doing publicity for special events, technology has made it much easier for them to start a small business than ever before.

Again, it is better to do something rather than nothing at all. Even if the business fails, grads can still learn something and have experience to put on their resume. And if the business is successful, it could turn into a dream job where the grad is the boss. For those who are risk-takers, don't mind working hard, and enjoy the freedom of working for themselves, being an entrepreneur could be the path to independence.

Coaching Tips to Help Millennials Make the Most of Their Experiences

- Don't underestimate the grads or their abilities—even if they have no formal qualifications, they will still have personal skills to offer.
- The company or organization they apply to or volunteer for should be chosen carefully, making sure that the experience will provide accomplishments that can be added to the resume and will improve the chances of getting into paid work.

Encourage your clients to:

- Be sensible about how much time they can realistically devote to the experience—it's not wise to offer more time than they can afford.
- Don't overlook small businesses, which offer a wide range of opportunities to develop skills and gain valuable experience.
- Network, network, network!
- Learn from co-workers; ask lots of questions.
- Keep a positive attitude and always do more than is expected.
- Try new things!

The twenties can be a time of growth and experimentation before the responsibilities of mid-life set in. So if your Millennial clients are still searching, encourage them to make the most of the journey.

Elise Oranges (Certified Professional Coach) has a B.A. from Marist College and received her coach training from Coach University. In addition to working with young people and those in transition, Elise has been in the publishing industry for 40 years, most recently as a quality analyst for an international company, as well as an adjunct instructor of copyediting at NYU and a publishing consultant. Elise is also a Reiki Master Teacher. She is the founder of Sunnywaters Coaching, a holistic life coaching practice. Elise lives in South Florida. For more information, visit her website: www.sunnywaterscoaching.com.

CHAPTER 11

CAN ASSESSMENT TESTS HELP?

By Carol Ann Vaughan

> *"I enjoyed working on the Myers-Briggs and Strengthsfinder.*
> *They helped me realize so many different things about myself. I*
> *now have a much more hopeful view towards life in general."*
> —MATTHEW

D o your clients sometimes wonder why some things are easy for them and other things are much more difficult? Do they wonder why some kinds of jobs appeal to them and others don't? Why some people are successful and others are not? Assessment tools can help a client identify his or her top talents—the innate strengths that enable one to do certain things better than others, the ones for which they exhibit the most ability and strongest interest. That awareness can make the difference between joy and success in a career and a difficult, unhappy slog.

Coaching Millennials often entails sorting through the many career options out there to find one for which they exhibit the most talent and strongest interest. Greater self-knowledge enables them to focus specifically on the careers for which they are most suited. Many do not understand the options they have and how their strengths and personality types can help them work most effectively to find the right fit.

Post-college Millennials who seek coaching are often struggling. Some have obtained jobs related to their major but are feeling disappointed. "I wish I'd majored in something else—I wish I could start over," they might say. Others have been unable to find any jobs at all or are underemployed in a job that doesn't require a degree. As a result, they often feel demoralized and question themselves and their choices. They begin to believe they are failures before they even launch their careers.

Assessments can provide valuable self-knowledge, which client and coach can use to identify careers that match the grad's strengths, skills, interests, and personality type. It is also very important in the coaching process to figure out what the young person is passionate about, because passion can fuel an ongoing sense of purpose and create resilience. For many Millennials, these assessments offer their first insights into who they really are as opposed to beliefs that they have developed about themselves from childhood. This is both extremely useful and very exciting for them.

There is a danger, though, when using testing which merely results in a list of job titles. Some of the choices offered will, in fact, appear to the young client to be totally unrealistic and improbable— for example, becoming an airplane pilot for someone who has a fear of flying or a graphic designer for someone with no art background.

Assessment tests are best considered as a point of departure for coaches to use their coaching skills. When going over the results of testing, listen carefully to your client, particularly noting the blocks she may have in selecting, applying, or interviewing for jobs. Attentively tuning in to your client and asking intuitively powerful questions are key to understanding what kind of support and coaching your client needs. So asking probing questions such as, "What would you be doing if money, education or current circumstances were irrelevant and you could not fail?" "Why are you drawn to this?"

and "What is stopping you from moving forward?"are essential to the process. Help the Millennial put together his or her own mosaic of choices, using the assessment as one tool to get the answers.

Tools and Choices

There are dozens of instruments and tools that coaches can use in assessing clients. No single test offers a one-stop answer for grads, but many can provide helpful information and important guidance. There are three that I've used effectively with young Millennials: 1. Myers-Briggs Type Indicator (MBTI®); 2. Humanmetrics-Jung Typology Test; and 3. StrengthsFinder®. In addition, I'm including two that were recommended by other coaches in the Grad Life Choices program: Assessment for Career Changers© by Juhua Wu; and the Seligman Optimism Test from the University of Pennsylvania. Coaches have also mentioned using the Holland Code and the Birkman Personality Assessment in helping clients assess their personality, interests, skills, and occupational aptitudes.

1. Myers-Briggs Type Indicator (MBTI®)

The MBTI®, developed by Isabel Myers and Katharine Briggs, is a measurement based on Carl Jung's theory of psychological or personality types. It identifies "psychological preferences"—preferred attitudes—rather than skills or abilities. It can help the client evaluate job-related environments that would be the best fit, as well as how they deal with interpersonal relationships (such as the relationship with a manager and co-workers), and how they can communicate most effectively, especially during times of stress and conflict.

The MBTI gives a client's natural preferences in four domains. Each domain shows two opposing pairs of preferences along a continuum. The following explanations of the four domains are adapted from the Myers-Briggs Foundation website, http://www.myersbriggs.org/my-mbti-personality-type/mbti-basics/.

E—I
Extroversion-Introversion (Do we get our energy from the outer world or from our own inner world?)

S—N
Sensing-Intuition (Do we focus on the basic information we take in or do we prefer to interpret and add meaning?)

T—F
Thinking-Feeling (When making decisions, do we prefer to first look at logic and consistency or at the people and circumstances involved?)

J—P
Judging-Perceiving (In dealing with the outside world, do we prefer to get things decided or do we prefer to stay open to new information and options?)

The MBTI is often provided at colleges and universities at a cost that varies from institution to institution. It requires a trained interpreter to help the client understand the results. With a deeper understanding of their personality type and approach to life, clients are better equipped to use their natural gifts and preferences to help them find a career.

Susan, a young woman I was coaching, believed that she could not network effectively since she was not an extrovert. After taking the MBTI, she realized that being an introvert simply meant that she derived her energy from being alone. So she realized that while she definitely could (and should) go out and network, she would need to make sure she gave herself time alone afterward to recoup her energy. She also uncovered through the MBTI that she was highly intuitive. She realized that using intuition (interpreting events and creating meaning) was a strong preference for her and that she should listen to it when making decisions about her career. As an intuitive introvert with writing ability, Susan looked into becoming a web editor as a potential career choice.

2. Humanmetrics.com/Jung Typology Test

Humanmetrics is an online instrument that is provided free to the user. This is a shorter, user-friendly alternative to the MBTI. It also offers a "type formula," a description of each personality type, and the specific strength of each preference. Like the MBTI, the Jung Typology Test helps identify where we get our energy, how we take in information, how we make decisions, and how we prefer to live every day. After taking the test, the client also obtains a list of the most suitable career choices based on personality. The individual's score and description of results give an overview of the client's personality, approach to decision-making and interpersonal relationships, and very general suggestions as to career possibilities.

Both the MBTI and Humanmetrics show each of the preferences on a continuum; therefore, one can see that preferences are rarely black and white. My client Robert was interested to discover that his placement on this continuum for extroversion was just slightly more than his preference for introversion, which explained why he needed more alone time than other extroverts. In addition, his other scores alerted him to the fact that while he had great interpersonal and salesmanship skills, he was apt to neglect his own needs for the needs of others. This knowledge helped him focus on moving toward his own goals rather than letting others interrupt him with their priorities. Click on: www.humanmetrics.com/

3. StrengthsFinder®

StrengthsFinder® provides an assessment of the client's five most powerful talent themes. The StrengthsFinder profile is the product of a 30-year, multimillion dollar effort by the Gallup organization to identify the most prevalent human strengths. The research included a systematic study of excellence. More than two million individual interviews were conducted with the best of the best performers. The assessment introduces 34 dominant "themes" with thousands of possible combinations, and reveals how these themes can best be translated into personal and career success. This assessment helps clients identify areas that would be good career choices, helps them describe themselves in a resume, and also provides them with language to describe their strengths in an interview.

In coaching Millennials, I find using the StrengthsFinder tool to be very effective. Identifying their top five talents enables clients to understand their deepest strengths and how to use them effectively. Since the job search can often be a demoralizing experience, the StrengthsFinder assessment empowers a young person to feel confident about his or her abilities. I often combine the StrengthsFinder assessment with either the MBTI or Humanmetrics: Jung Typology Test (free online) to give grads a full picture of their strengths, where they get energy, how they take in information, how they make decisions, and how they tend to deal with the world. These insights reveal the client's basic approach to life.

In the event that a coach has not had StrengthsFinder training, a number of materials are available on the website (www.gallup-strengthscenter.com) that help clients in the understanding of their talents. These materials, which are also included at a cost, are the Signature Theme Report, Insight Report Guide, Strengths Insight & Action Planning Guide, and Ideas for Action.

As a coach, I trained with Gallup and received my coach certification from them in 2007. Even without training, however, most life coaches would be able to review these materials on the website and be able to use them with a client in the context of coaching around careers.

How Knowing Your Strengths Can Help

Jack, a young client who had been criticized for appearing to have no clear goals (and started to worry about this characteristic), took the StrengthsFinder test and was excited to find that Adaptability (the ability to easily move from one project to the other) was a dominant strength for him. It did not mean that he lacked goals, only that he was able to shift gears when necessary more easily than other people. This was a talent that he could translate into a job skill as a project manager.

Laura, who was demoralized by her job search, was happy to discover through StrengthsFinder that she had strengths in Positivity and Discipline. This led her to conclude that, among the fields she was considering, sales and marketing would be a great fit. She promptly revised her resume and LinkedIn profile to reflect these talents and strengths. She gained self-esteem by knowing what her strengths were and was able to present herself confidently at her next interview.

4. Self-Assessment for Job Seekers© by Juhua Wu

Created by life and career coach Juhua Wu, this self-assessment works around a 15-domain scale to get an idea of the state of the client's personal and professional development and indicates the areas in which the client needs support. This assessment does not seek to uncover specific strengths or abilities; instead it indicates how satisfied the client is with different aspects of his or her life. It can be administered during coaching at six-week intervals to help the coach and client assess how the client is progressing in coaching. It's a way to measure growth in the areas the client would like to work on.

QUICK ASSESSMENT
FOR CAREER CHANGERS AND JOB SEEKERS
BY JUHUA WU

On a scale of 1-10, 10 being the most optimal and satisfying state, 1 being the worst and least satisfying state, please rate the following: (select only the relevant ones for each client)

DOMAIN	Week 1	Week 6	Week 12
1. Current job situation (like your job)			
2. Body/Physical Health			
3. Emotions/Mental Health			
4. Work-life Balance			
5. Financial situation			
6. Relationships—Intimate/close			
7. Relationships—others			
8. Confidence			
9. Self-perception (like being oneself)			
10. Self-trust			
11. Motivation for career move			
12. Motivation in general			
13. Professional skills/self-development			
14. Job search/career transition skills			
15. Resilience/ability to deal with stress & challenges			

©Juhua Wu 2017

5. Optimism Test

This test, created by Dr. Martin Seligman, who is known as the "father of Positive Psychology," identifies the client's level of optimism. The test registers the degree to which people see the cup as half empty or half full, which affects how resilient and resourceful they will be in the face of adversity. Optimists look at problems as challenges to overcome, not as permanent stumbling blocks. They view failure as temporary and don't attribute it to their own deficiencies. So they tend to bounce back when bad things happen. By contrast, pessimists view problems as permanent, pervasive, and personal, which tends to make them less resilient. Fortunately, pessimists can learn to notice and improve their explanatory style, which can help them weather inevitable stresses. This test gives the coach insight into how the client perceives his or her level of hopefulness. It may be a predictor of how the client will handle the job search. This 32-question assessment is available free online on the University of Pennsylvania's Authentic Happiness website: https://www.authentichappiness.sas.upenn.edu/questionnaires/optimism-test

Self-Understanding Enhances the Job Search Process

To recap, by using assessment tools and testing in conjunction with intuitively powerful questions, coaches can enable young people to:

1. Understand and identify their strengths, skills, and personality style, which helps them identify areas that would be good career choices. A client should ask herself or himself: Is this job one that will allow me to use my strengths and abilities? Is this an environment where I can thrive?
2. Develop the language to describe their strength and abilities in powerful ways on both their resumes and in job

interviews. For instance, using the job description provided by the employer, young people will be able to customize their resumes to reflect how they can perform the responsibilities required and how they have used these strengths and abilities in the past to accomplish goals. Applicants will be able to paint a picture of who they are and what they can accomplish. They will feel more confident talking about their strengths while networking and in job interviews.

One of my Millennial clients, Gretchen, was an unemployed sociology major. Based on her assessment testing and discussions during our coaching sessions, she decided to go after an entry-level job as an HR generalist. An excellent opportunity arose with a large multinational company. During the interview, she was asked to tell the HR manager about herself. Later, she excitedly told me that instead of just saying, "I'm good with people," she was able to share a richer and more detailed self-assessment: "I have the ability to sense what people are feeling and articulate it. I have the ability to help people reach consensus." She had prepared a couple of examples of *how* she used these strengths in college projects and jobs. Her assessments helped her feel confident in describing her abilities during the interview—and it showed. Within two weeks, Gretchen shared with me the great news: she got the position and launched her career!

Carol Ann Vaughan (Certified Professional Coach) received her comprehensive coach training at Accomplishment Coaching. She has more than 30 years' experience in high school, community college, university and nonprofit education environments, including 12 years working specifically in the areas of student services. Carol received a B.A. in education from Arizona State University where she graduated cum laude, and has completed extensive graduate work. She currently runs her own coaching company, What's Next Coaching, where she works with clients on personal and career development. Carol lives in San Diego, CA. To learn more about Carol, visit her website at www.whatsnextcoaching.net.

PART III: JOB SEARCH ESSENTIALS

CHAPTER 12

CREATING GREAT RÉSUMÉS AND COVER LETTERS FOR TODAY'S CHANGING JOB MARKET

By Greg Lewis

> *"I no longer undervalue myself. In fact, each resume*
> *I update looks stronger, highlighting my experience*
> *and creating significant value to me."*
> —ANDREW

The statistics don't lie, but they are constantly changing. As Baby Boomers move into retirement, the largest influx into the marketplace has been the Millennial generation, which represents those born between about 1982 and 2004 (Strauss and Howe, 2000). While Millennials have been characterized in a variety of ways, one thing is certainly true: they are willing to change jobs often in search of something they perceive as more fulfilling or interesting. The result can be a work history of multiple jobs lasting only 1-3 years per organization. Generally, recruiters consider such "job-hopping" to be a red flag when vetting candidates. But the consistent movement among Millennials may force employers to reconsider their approach.

From my perspective as a longtime career development expert, I've seen hiring become less about the job history and more about the candidate's experience and skills obtained during the time in the workforce. The goal for Millennials is to develop their branding around the relevant skills and experience needed for a particular industry or position. The personal brand individuals create when marketing themselves to employers typically includes a resume, a cover letter, and a social media presence (e.g. LinkedIn, Facebook, Twitter, and whatever platform comes next). The focus for this chapter will be the resume and cover letter components of the Millennial's personal brand. From research on the company to following up on an application, there are several best practices that can help young people navigate these aspects of the job search process.

The Key to a Great Resume: Make It Relevant

While there are many important features in a resume that might get your Millennial client the interview, the focus here will be on two critical factors.

Regardless of how many jobs a young professional has had, the key to a winning resume is developing a readable format and tailoring the resume to the position the individual is seeking. A common mistake for job seekers is to use the same resume to apply for a variety of positions, sometimes within the same organization. Recruiters or computerized applicant tracking systems (ATS) will easily recognize generic resumes, and the applicant's chances are likely over before he or she even gets started.

As a career services specialist at a university, I work with students from ages 18 to 70. What do most of these job seekers have in common? They seek employment through online job boards by uploading the same resume to each site. While it is understandable that your client would not want to create dozens of resumes, the reality is that posting in this fashion just doesn't work. In fact, depending on the statistics you refer to, 80-90% of job seekers apply online while only 10% of jobs are found that way. Does that seem like a successful approach?

There was a time when you could call an employer directly to inquire about a position or to follow up on your application. No more. In today's market, an applicant using a generic resume will receive only a "received" email but little else. Given these circumstances, the importance of doing your research before developing your marketing documents is critical. Here are the most useful strategies to share with your Millennial clients.

First, start with the posted job description. This will dictate how to develop the resume to fit the position. This doesn't mean that they need a brand-new resume for every job they pursue—it usually just means they need to tailor or adapt their resume for the position described. The job description will identify the skills, competencies, education, and experience needed for a particular position. The resume's goal is two-fold: to use the search terms that will get through the computerized automated tracking system, or ATS (software programs that scan resumes to identify keywords that match the job description), and to convince the recruiter the client has most of the priority requirements for the role. While a bit old-school, I advise my clients to print a hard copy of the job description and highlight the specific parts of the description that seem most important. When completing this exercise, always consider it from the point of view of the employer/recruiter:

- What is the problem they seek to solve by hiring someone into this role?
- What is the biggest need to be met for someone to be successful in this position?
- What skills and competencies are critical for the job?

The initial step of identifying what the employer wants and needs will help the applicant with the next step—identifying aspects of their professional background that qualify them for the position. The challenge for Millennials is to reflect on their various experiences and determine which job duties, accomplishments, and acquired skills match the job. Successful applicants are those who take the time to align their resume to match the job description with their relevant background. To provide a simple example of what this might look like, take a look at the following: a sample job description and a resume that highlights the relevant skills needed for the role.

Job Description: Sales Manager

EXPERIENCE: Must have at least two years of sales experience with strong customer service skills.

REQUIRED SKILLS: Must be proficient in needs-based sales techniques. Must be able to communicate and coordinate a team effectively and work with an extremely high degree of accuracy. Individual must be able to work independently without direct supervision from regional manager, and work well under pressure.

DUTIES: Perform a variety of substantive sales and managerial duties, including quarterly reviews, weekly sales reports, and interacting with customers and staff.

EDUCATION: A four-year degree from a regionally accredited college or university, or an Associate's degree with five years of experience.

Sample Resume Customized to Align with Job Description
Customer Service Representative
XYZ Company, Atlanta, GA   July 2014-present

- Provide excellent customer service by attending to clients' questions and concerns in an efficient manner.
- Communicate with customers, executives, and vendors regarding possible issues and resolutions.
- Coordinate multiple projects concurrently with little to no supervision.
- Perform various tasks such as preparing proposals, managing sales territory, and maintaining accuracy in tracking and reporting of sales data.

Note how some of the skills on the job description are repeated in the resume. While not a perfect match, this is an example of how one can identify skills acquired from previous jobs and translate them into a resume for a specific opportunity.

Another component that will help Millennials tailor their resumes to the position is to include a *Career Title and Skills Summary* at the top of their resume, under their contact information. According to a study conducted by Ladders.com (2012), most recruiters spend only 6-10 seconds on average reviewing a resume. This statistic underscores the importance of clearly identifying the position you seek and your related skills that would attract the interest of the reviewer. A career title with related skills is an excellent way to communicate your relevant competencies at the top of your resume. Instead of the usual "job objective" statement, which is often vague and similar to what your competition will use, a career title will tell a hiring manager exactly what job you seek and how you are qualified for the position.

Here's an example below of what the *Career Title and Skills Summary* might look like:

Customer Service Specialist / Community Service Coordinator

- Training and mentoring
- Community relations
- Multi-line telephone
- Report writing
- Relationship development
- Event coordination
- Fluent in Spanish
- Inside Sales
- Excel and PowerPoint

The Career Title should be altered for each job and the bulleted keywords should reflect skills that match the job title. Keywords make it easy for the reader to identify qualifications, and of course they improve the candidate's chances of getting through any computerized ATS.

Note: Each time you send out your resume, be sure to proofread to correct any spelling or syntax errors that might have crept in. This can easily happen when a resume is customized for a new job application.

When You Lack Experience

Relevant coursework: Another resume strategy for recent grads might be to include relevant coursework under their "Education section." When you lack experience or are looking to break into a new industry, establishing your educational credentials can help make you a viable candidate. The inclusion of 4-6 courses can enhance your resume for a recruiter. The example below shows what this might look like:

XYZ University, New York, NY
Bachelor of Science in Business Administration–Management June 2016

Relevant Coursework:

- Marketing
- Business Ethics
- Accounting
- Finance
- HR Management
- Business Law

Community involvement: Think about other experiences outside of work history. Summer jobs, internships, college activities, and volunteer work are all valuable in developing an individual's skills. Millennials should reflect on their involvement in activities that may not have much or any paycheck involved when revising their resume. The key, as always, is to keep it as relevant as possible. For example, the individual below is interested in breaking into the healthcare administration field with no paid experience. However, she does have practical volunteer experience and should certainly list this prominently on her resume.

Office Volunteer   October 2010 –Present
American Cancer Society

- Make outbound calls to solicit donations for cancer research
- Coordinate volunteer schedules for events ranging from 50–2000 people
- Developed and implemented an electronic filing system to improve the tracking of donations and facilitate consistent donor relations

Where possible, your client should include specific successful projects they have worked on, especially if they can show concrete results.

Use a Readable Format

In addition to having the clients tailor their skills, education, and experience to the position they seek, it is important to format the resume so the reader can easily identify the needed information. Here's how the *Experience* section should look on a resume. Keeping in mind the Ladders.com study, the resume must be clean and easy to read so recruiters don't have to hunt for the information they need. Recruiters will not waste time looking for how or why the applicant is qualified, so don't underestimate the importance of design and format. To demonstrate how this can make the difference between moving on in the process or a rejection email, note the differences in the "before" and "after" versions of a job experience listed on a resume:

Before:
Marketing Assistant   March 2016-Present
XYZ Inc. Mascoutah, IL
I manage all company social media marketing programs. In particular, I research, develop and post effective email blasts, blogs, and ads. Provide additional administrative support and data entry for various marketing projects.

After:
Marketing Assistant   March 2016-Present
XYZ Inc., Mascoutah, IL
Manage all company social media marketing campaigns.

- Created a Facebook page for the company's charity auction, which had 11,000 visitors.
- Research and develop email blasts, blogs, and ads for external posting.
- Produced an ad campaign that resulted in $50,000 in new business.
- Provide administrative support and data entry for marketing projects.
- Proficient in Microsoft Excel, PowerPoint, and Word

Creating a Winning Cover Letter

The purpose of a cover letter is to communicate to a potential employer why you're the best candidate for the position based on your skills, education, and experience. Cover letters are generally three to four paragraphs long and, again, should be tailored to the position the grad is seeking.

Some employers use cover letters to determine a person's ability to write. The following steps will help the grad prepare for writing a cover letter:

Step 1: Review the job description and highlight important skills and qualifications that the employer is seeking.

Step 2: Write down all the skills the grad possesses that match the skills in the description.

Step 3: Pick 3-4 of these skills and emphasize them in the cover letter.

Step 4: Give examples of when and where you used or obtained those 3 to 4 skills (drawn from jobs or experiences listed on the resume).

Cover Letter Checklist:

1. Give your contact information.
2. Give the contact information of the employer you are contacting.
3. Address a person by name whenever possible. This is usually available on LinkedIn.
4. Tell them why you are writing and demonstrate some knowledge of their company.
5. Using your three skills and examples, tell them why you are qualified for the position. Emphasize what you can deliver in the role.
6. Thank them for their time, and tell them what you want to happen next.
7. Proofread to make sure there are no spelling or syntax errors.

8. Make the letter engaging and memorable, using some personal detail that might help you stand out.

Below is an example of what a successful cover letter might look like:

SAMPLE	COVER LETTER
1. List your contact information.	Your Name, Address, Phone, Email Today's Date
2. List the information for the employer you are contacting.	Company Name Address
3. Address a person by name whenever possible.	Dear (Name of Recruiter/ Hiring Manager),
4. Tell them why you are writing and demonstrate some knowledge of their company.	I am excited to apply to the Association Membership Administration position with XYZ company, which I found on Indeed.com. It would be an honor to work for an organization that is so dedicated to improving health care and staying abreast of the latest research. Given my health care education and background, I feel I can make a positive contribution to XYZ organization.
5. Using your three skills and examples, tell them why you are qualified for the position.	In 2010, I completed my Bachelor of Science degree in Health Care Studies from University of Texas (Dallas). Through my undergraduate experience, I was able to obtain a strong foundation in the sciences and a deep understanding of the U.S. health care system and current obstacles and challenges the health care industry is facing. As the Program Coordinator at Memorial Hospital, I regularly built relationships with both internal and external customers. I formed collaborative partnerships with several community organizations and doubled participation in our outreach program. In addition to relationship building, I honed my database management skills while serving as an Administrative Assistant at GE. In this role, I utilized PeopleSoft to manage clients' information.
6. Thank them for their time and tell them what you want to happen next.	I would like the opportunity to discuss this position and my qualifications in greater detail. Thank you in advance for your time and consideration. Best regards, Jane M. Doe

Given the fact that Millennials are likely to have many jobs and/or careers, consider recommending that they develop a "master" resume that includes all of their employment history to keep track of their skills, education, and experience. As they move forward in their career, it is pivotal to update their resume periodically to assure they have saved a record of their career development. However, to be successful in the job search, job seekers must be willing to create resumes and cover letters that are unique to each job they seek.

As young people develop their resumes and cover letters, the key is not to focus on what they may be lacking from a direct experience perspective but rather to highlight the skills and qualifications they offer a potential employer. With this mindset, Millennials can communicate their varied skill set, strengths, knowledge, and passion to make a difference through their work.

Greg Lewis is a veteran career advisor working with students and alumni at National University. In addition to his focus on advising veterans, active military and military spouses, Greg works to develop relationships with companies interested in hiring National University students and alumni. He has a B.A. degree in history from Santa Clara University and a master's degree from San Diego State University in Post-Secondary Educational Leadership with a concentration in Student Affairs. Greg lives in San Diego, CA.

CHAPTER 13

HELPING GRADS ACE THEIR JOB INTERVIEWS

By Susan Hay and Emily Benson

> *"My interviewing skills are an obstacle to getting a job because I lack confidence in my abilities and experience."*
> —MEGAN

Sending your Millennial client off to his or her first interview while under your guidance is a pivotal moment in the relationship between client and coach. This is the test—is your coaching paying off? Can clients take what you have taught them and apply it to the nerve-wracking interview experience? You won't be there to hold your client's hand, and the stakes are high. At LaunchingU we specialize in helping recent college grads get started in the workplace. In this chapter we cover our overall philosophy of interviewing and why it's so hard for entry-level candidates. We discuss how to help your young clients prepare for the interview, apply for jobs, and do well at their first interviews. We also discuss how to debrief with your clients afterward in order to learn from and improve the interviewing experience.

Before we explore the challenges and excitement of coaching young college grads through their first "real" interviews, we assume you've already worked with your clients through identifying their strengths, values, and possible career choices, as well as helped them to learn how to make connections in an interview between their skills and interests and the industries, organizations, and jobs to which they're applying. Their career materials (resume and cover letter) must also be polished and professional, and effectively convey their accomplishments and skills.

It's equally important to work with them to shape *meaningful past success stories*. This is essential to helping to build their confidence and understand their strengths and weaknesses. As you'll see below, these success stories (also called "accomplishment stories") will play a major role in the interviewing process.

The Post-College Grad: A Major Shift in Identity

Coaching young people through their transition into the professional world is deeply meaningful work. Our clients are going through one of life's major shifts, and in our experience this involves much more than learning new career skills and buying new clothes. It is an entire shift in identity—from college student to young professional. We work with our clients to draw out their past experiences and future plans, so they can talk about what has been most valuable with confidence and authority. Then we "basc coach" them through networking, relationship building, and informational interviews so they can try on their more confident, professional personas. This process can be a painful one for many young adults. They don't yet know how to embody their new identities. The clothes feel uncomfortable, the small talk is forced, and they can feel awkward, almost like imposters posing as adults.

During the precarious process of shifting identities from college to the work world, an interview for a "real" job becomes a matter of serious importance. For better or worse, interviews consistently test our clients the most. No one likes to be judged and rejected, but the fear is heightened for those who are young and inexperienced. A positive interview—one that they have prepared for and feel good about—can be a big confidence booster, whether or not they get the job. A poor interviewing experience, on the other hand, can be a huge setback.

Wherever our clients are in the process of career development and job hunting, when they first begin working with us we typically ask them to press the pause button on sending out resumes or going out on interviews. They often need to do some fundamental work; otherwise they will experience unconstructive or non-responses and will wind up more frustrated and cynical. Rejection in the professional world is hard for all of us. We teach our clients how not to make the same mistakes twice and learn from their difficult experiences.

After we have asked our clients to take a break from applying for jobs, we dive in with them to find out who they are and where they are in terms of understanding themselves and the types of careers they are envisioning for themselves. If their experience until then has been negative or harsh, we reframe it with them that "of course it was like that—they weren't prepared—but they will be by the time they do the next interview."

Preparing for Interviews: Essential Steps

When we are finally ready to start preparing for actual interviews, we push our clients hard—to prepare, prepare, prepare. We want them to go into a professional interview as a future colleague and peer, not as a college student visiting a world they don't understand (or at least to be able to fake it!).

1. Telling the Accomplishment Story: The first way we prepare grads for interviews is to help them identify their accomplishment stories. They all have them, but they often do not know how to artic-ulate them yet. We work with clients to identify their top three to five accomplishment stories early in our work together, as these form the backbone of their resumes—but they are also critically important in the interview process.

For our clients, understanding their accomplishments is the foun-dation of being able to do well in a *behavioral interview*. Behavioral interviewing is based on the idea that the best predictor of future impact will be examples of prior impact. Not all interviewers are good at this kind of interview, or even understand it, but it is a best practice in the field of interviewing and recruiting. Even when the interviewer doesn't use this approach, clients will benefit from mas-tering it. It's a very effective way of answering almost any question at an interview. Grads need to practice telling their accomplishment stories with their coach so that they sound natural and are comfort-able applying them to questions the interviewer might ask.

1. Explain the SITUATION that your accomplishment is embedded in.
2. Describe the TASKS associated with the accomplishments and the ACTIONS you took.
3. Communicate the RESULTS you achieved in the situation.

Interview questions that are coming from a behavioral perspective typically start out, "Please give me an example of a time where you _____." Here's a sample answer:

Interviewer: "Can you give me an example of a time when you went above and beyond expectations in a job?"

Interviewee: "Certainly. I needed to work throughout col-lege, and one of the jobs that I could fit into my academic schedule was as a salesperson at a big box retailer in the sports equipment/apparel market. It was a pretty boring job, and they had very low expectations of their team. To make it more interesting, I asked my boss if there was a way I could learn more about the products—athletic shoes.

"My boss showed me where to go on their link to the different key manufacturers and learn about how they differentiated their shoes from their competitors. For the next couple of weeks, on my breaks and lunch hour, I studied these products, learned how to sell them more effectively, and why we were displaying them in specific ways. A few weeks into this, my boss made me the lead on my shifts in that department, and then started bringing me into meetings about what shoes were selling well and why. Before the semester was out, they offered me a manager's position in the store and an opportunity to be part of their management training program. Because of my school situation, and because I was not really targeting a career in retail, I had to turn them down, but I continued to take every opportunity to learn more about our products. I became a very strong sales representative, and my boss at that store is one of my references today."

2. Going Over the Likely Questions: Once clients fully understand behavioral interviewing, we share a list of questions that they are likely to face as they begin interviewing, and we ask them to write out their answers. The writing process helps them connect more deeply with these answers. We then review the answers and help them improve them—always focusing on getting them to connect their accomplishment stories to the question they are being asked.

This process can go on for several sessions depending on how quickly they pick it up. We know they are ready when they are in active story-telling mode in their answers. Then it is time for them to go live.

3. Mock Interviews: We set up mock interviews with key people who have an HR or recruiting background. As part of the preparation process, we use a job description online that the client chooses and we agree that they would candidate for that job. We share that job description with the interviewer. We ask the interviewer to pay specific attention to:

- How well the client establishes a connection with them during the interview.
- How well they bring their own accomplishments into play as they are answering specific questions.

We ask the interviewers to give the candidate feedback at the end of the interview but to use the *compliment sandwich* when they are doing it. By this we mean that they should figure out the two or three biggest areas the candidate can improve on, but find two things to compliment for every one thing that needs improvement. The interviewer can then share more things with us directly regarding areas for improvement than they explored with the client.

After the first mock interview, we do more work with clients to incorporate the feedback into their approach to an interview, and then we set up a second interview with a different interviewer. This one is face-to-face if geography allows, but if not, it is typically a Skype interview. Again, we ask for feedback from the interviewer. Typically by the second interview, grads are much more competent and therefore much more comfortable. This is definitely a skill that improves with practice. Practice breeds competency, which breeds comfort, which reinforces competency. In some cases, more practice is necessary, and we keep them going until we believe they are ready.

From Job Application to Real, Live Interview

When our clients identify jobs they want to apply for, we teach them how to tweak their resume and cover letter for specific job openings. We also teach them about applicant tracking systems (ATS) and the importance of using keywords in their resume and cover letter.

And then – *BAM*!– sometimes quickly and sometimes later than they would like, the grad gets an email or a call that a given company wants to talk with them or meet with them for a specific opportunity! This is a moment that creates excitement and panic. As coaches, we are in the mode of helping our client calm down and get back to preparing for an interview.

We go over with them how to research that specific company and the specific role, and how to break down a company website to be conversant with the business, the direction, key initiatives, values, etc. We help them look up the key people in the organization who will interview them. And we go back over the job description and help them remember *why* they would be a good candidate and *how* their accomplishments, experience, and interests are a good fit for a role like this. This phase of the work is really about steadying the clients, helping them stay confident and on their game as they head into the interview.

Nailing the Entry-Level Interview

In many professional job interviews, the interviewee is trying to prove that he or she has the specific skills that a job requires, plus deep knowledge and experience. For entry-level job applicants, however, it is often the case that the interviewees do not have direct experience in the jobs for which they are applying. In this situation, the goals of the interview are different. For entry-level job interviews, applicants need to show *work ethic, deep curiosity, and excitement*, and they need to *connect their past experiences to the specific job they are interviewing for*.

We ask them to set goals for the interview as they are preparing. What do they want to make sure the interviewer knows about them? What do they want to learn about the organization?

Interview Etiquette, Clothing, Handshake: At an interview your Millennial client's new "young professional" identity will be tested. Your clients are most likely not totally comfortable dressing and acting like professionals, and they may need more coaching than you think. For example, you will be surprised how many of them need help understanding what to wear on an interview—we actively coach our clients here. It helps to do it well before the interview to avoid the panic of "oh my God, I have to go out and buy a blazer!" We have found that we need to help them understand that it is better to be overdressed than underdressed. They are prone to being very embarrassed if they show up in a nice shirt and pants and a tie when everyone else is business casual. We tell them that this is normal— someone coming in for an interview should be dressed up, even in a casual office.

We don't assume that our clients are familiar with other aspects of the etiquette of interviewing. They are instructed not to wear perfume or cologne or chew gum, and not to smoke before the interview. We remind them to turn off their phones and never to check them during the interview, even if the interview gets interrupted. We make sure that they have a leather portfolio to carry with them, containing extra resumes, a notepad and pen to take notes, and a list of questions they have for the interviewer. We also coach them on keeping their energy level high and telling their stories in an engaging manner. For some clients this comes naturally, while for others it is much more difficult.

We have also found that our clients often need help with the handshake. It seems like such a small thing, but we have seen strong candidates lose out on opportunities they were qualified for because they didn't shake hands well. We ask them to shake our hand to get a sense of whether they understand how to do this properly. If you are coaching a client long-distance and therefore can't check this out yourself, we recommend that you have the client go to two people who have professional careers and ask them to evaluate their handshake.

Handshake Basics:

1. Face the other person directly at a socially normal distance apart.
2. Offer your whole hand, not just your fingers.
3. Look the person in the eyes, and keep eye contact long enough to know what color their eyes are.
4. Say, "I'm very happy to meet you," or "I'm so happy to see you again." Apply enough pressure to be firm, but don't squeeze too hard. A handshake should not be painful.

The key offenders in the world of bad handshakes are The Dead Fish and The Bone-crusher.

Questions to Ask at an Interview

A good interviewer will judge candidates almost as much on the questions they ask as on how they answer the interviewer's questions. We think it's important to help the grad prepare questions in advance. These questions should serve a number of purposes:

1. To demonstrate that the candidate has done his or her homework on the company. We work with our clients to go over the website of the company very carefully. We want to be sure they understand the business the company is in; how the company describes their values and mission, their culture, and their relationship with their customers; and any current news that is important enough that the company is highlighting it.

If the company is publicly traded, we ask them to look at the financials, and if it is a nonprofit, we ask that they look at the public information available regarding their financials. This deep dive helps them form a stronger opinion regarding their interest in the company and also suggests a few important questions they can ask. Examples of relevant questions might include:

- How does your company distinguish itself from its direct competitors?
- I found your values to be very powerfully stated and aligned with what I am hoping to find in my first professional role out of college. How does the company bring these values to bear on the day-to-day work environment?
- I am interested in learning more about _____. (Fill in the blank with a company initiative or a press release, etc., that caught your eye as you were going through the website.)

2. To get more information on what is important to the interviewer/company so they can continue to sell themselves; and to gain more information on whether this job will be a good fit for them.

In addition to assessing a given candidate's skill level and experience, good interviewers are also trying to ferret out whether they will be a strong cultural fit with their organization. So we train our clients to ask questions that get to values in the organization. One excellent question a candidate might ask: "What qualities tend to make people successful at Company X?"

This shows the interviewer that the candidate is focused on succeeding, and the answer will give the candidate insight into what leads to success in this company. If the answer is some version of: "We have found that people who are self-starters, who don't need a tremendous amount of guidance and who figure out how to add value do well here"—then a candidate could bring up the instance when she went "above and beyond expectations" and reinforce why this company is probably a good fit for her. She can say that this company has the kind of culture that she wants to work in. She could mention that being a self-starter is a trait that runs through her work history and that her references would highlight that about her as an employee.

On the other hand, the answer might be some version of: "We tend to value employees who do whatever it takes to get the job done and are willing to work 60 + hours a week on a regular basis." If in our values testing, the Millennial client listed work-life balance as one of his or her most important variables when considering a job, we would help the grad to prepare a more neutral answer. For instance, they might state that they are very dedicated to bringing strong results and have learned how to work smartly and efficiently to produce those results in their prior workplaces. Meanwhile, the grad has also learned very important information that may make this potential opportunity less interesting.

Other questions that make sense for candidates to ask of a potential hiring manager include:

1. In this role, who would my key interfaces be and what is currently most important to them?

2. What concerns do you have about the department/organization/business today and how could the employee in this role help allay your concerns?
3. What kind of results/deliverables do you expect to see from this position in the first six months?

These are first-round interview questions. As important as it is to ask the right questions, it is equally important to not ask the wrong questions in a first interview. For example, the first interview is not the place to ask about compensation. In general, candidates want to keep the focus on what the company/interviewer needs from them so that they can do the best possible job of presenting themselves as an irresistible candidate. In a second interview, should they get there, they can ask other questions such as:

- How will you onboard the person you hire into this role?
- Would it be possible to talk with someone who is relatively close to my level in the company, who has joined the company within the last 12 months?
- What kinds of developmental opportunities or training would I receive during my first year?

There are also questions that you just don't ever want to ask. Period. Here are a few of them.

The No-Nos

1. Do not ask a question that can easily be answered by doing a quick Google search.

2. Do not ask how quickly you can be promoted.
3. Do not ask whether the company does background checks.
4. Do not ask about gossip you may have heard about the company.

If our clients like what they learned about the company during the interview, we encourage them to tell their interviewer that they want the job and explain why. Everyone, including HR professionals and hiring managers, loves to be loved—so telling them that you want to join them is a powerful move. Include in your "ask" some specifics about what you like about the team and the organization and how you see your skills as a good fit.

Answering the Most Common (and Scariest) Questions

There are two questions that are not behavioral questions, but almost ALWAYS get asked and seem to be the scariest for our clients: "Tell me about yourself," and "What's your greatest weakness?" We spend a lot of time coaching our clients on these two particular questions, and our clients spend time practicing their answers.

1. Tell me about yourself. What makes this question so hard for this cohort group is that it calls up the identity shift young college grads must go through. To answer this question, they have to learn to talk about themselves as a young professional— not just a college student. The answer to this question needs to be focused on storytelling about one or two specific college and work accomplishments, and should address why your client applied to the job he or she is now interviewing for. If possible, they should mention their passion for the field, as demonstrated through something they've done in the past. This is also a good place for an interviewee to tell a story that illustrates a past success through the eyes of someone else, e.g., "Well, I think my former boss/friends would tell you that I am…"

Here's how one of our clients might have answered this question:

"I grew up in the suburbs of Connecticut in a blue-collar family. My father is a police officer and my mother works in administration in our local high school. I worked all through high school and much of college in a landscaping company, and by the time I left I was the right-hand person for the owner, independently working with customers and managing work crews.

"I have always been impressed with the work of fire departments and became a cadet firefighter in high school. I have pursued as much training as possible during my work with my local fire department, and I am proud of the fact that I became a volunteer firefighter last year.

"I came to _____ college because of its strong program in workplace safety. I want my career to involve improving the safety of employees and potentially consumers. I am proud of the fact that I have maintained a 3.3 GPA overall and a 3.5 in my major and that I have done that while working 20 hours a week throughout college.

"I know I am a hard worker, and I thrive in situations where I can be part of a team and where I have significant responsibility. I have good communication skills, I am a self-starter, and I am so ready to get started in my career!"

2. What's your greatest weakness? There are two good ways for an entry-level job candidate to answer this question. The first is to mention the fact that this will be their first "real" job. For example, "Well, I would say that my biggest weakness currently is that I am relatively new to the professional world, and I recognize there will be a learning curve when I begin my career." They should then turn this line of thinking around and talk about the internship and/or work experience they *do* have that has prepared them (to some extent) for their new professional role. Another possible answer is for the interviewee to pick a particular skill (e.g., using software that they know the company uses) and talk about how they will need to get up to speed on that skill. They should talk about how they have learned a similar skill in the past, and that they are confident in their abilities to learn quickly.

Another approach is to take a true but non-catastrophic example and then talk about what they have done to overcome it. For example, "I don't love public speaking. I used to get nervous if I had to speak in front of a group. I decided that I was just plain tired of being so nervous, and I actually went to Toast Masters for several months. I have to say that they have an amazing process for helping with this issue, and I now am confident that I know how to organize and present on most any topic.

"It's still not my favorite thing to do. But I have overcome the anxiety that kept me from being able to do it credibly, and I actually look for opportunities to present on a small scale, so I can stay confident."

Debriefing After the Interview

We recommend debriefing with your Millennial clients as quickly as possible after the interviews. We like to talk to them when the experience is still very fresh and before the always present internal spin doctor takes over and sways their perspective. We go through each interview and ask in some detail for them to talk about the questions asked, how they answered them, how they felt in the process, and what they liked and did not like about the information they received during the interview. We ask for descriptive answers versus evaluative ones. For example, we will ask them what they thought was their best answer and which one they felt they could have improved upon.

Any time they offer judgments regarding how they did or what they thought about the people they met, we ask them to use data to make their point. We are attempting to help them see each interview as a learning opportunity from which they can determine where they did well and how they could improve next time.

Your clients should write down the names of everyone they met in the interview and collect business cards if possible. Doing so facilitates their sending emails later on to thank them for their time and restating their interest in the role. By "later on" we mean within 24 hours! In our background as HR leaders, we were always surprised when candidates didn't do this. It is always noticed, and when someone doesn't send a follow-up thank-you email, it is seen as either a lack of interest or a lack of professionalism. Neither attribute is one we would want for our clients.

Ideally your client will send a separate email to each person with whom they interviewed and personalize it as much as possible. They can personalize it by commenting favorably on something the interviewer shared with them about what he or she loves about the company or job. This is also an opportunity to mention something they forgot to bring up, or to very briefly elaborate on an answer they gave, if they feel it may have been incomplete or not fully articulated.

The Value of Coaching for Interview Success

Working with clients through the interview process is incredibly fun and exciting. Millennial clients will be testing their new professional identities and entering organizations as potential co-workers. Keeping their confidence high through the inevitable setbacks is the toughest part of this phase, but the payoff is massive. Interviewing skills are critical for career success; yet even many experienced professionals do not feel comfortable in interviews. Recent grads who can nail their interviews have a huge advantage over other job candidates. Coach your clients well through this challenging process, and before you know it, you will be coaching them through their first salary negotiation!

Susan Hay, M.A., and **Emily Benson**, Ph.D., are managing partners at LaunchingU, where they work with college students and new college graduates to help them launch their careers. Susan brings a successful career in executive-level human resources roles and in executive search to her coaching work. In addition to her role of managing partner at LaunchingU, Emily is an associate professor in management at Keene State College and had prior experience in human resources in the IT and construction industries. To learn more about Susan and Emily's coaching practice, visit their website at: www.launchingu.com.

CHAPTER 14

COACHING CRITICAL NETWORKING SKILLS

By Sandra Klein

> *"My inability to start a real career had become a serious depressant in my life. I became aware that networking was my greatest weakness in job hunting. Now I routinely attempt to network and reach out for help to everyone I know who seems happy and secure in their career."*
> —*LIAM*

Many grads have told me that they spend their days sending hundreds of resumes out to job postings and websites of potential employers. Yet most often they hear nothing back. What's going on?

They might be overlooking a key factor in job search today: networking. Why is networking so important? According to Ryan Raver, author of *A PhD's Complete Guide to Networking*: "Networking is responsible for 90% or more of finding employment, whereas cold resume submission has been reported as low as only 4-10%." In addition, in an interview on NPR's *All Things Considered*, Matt Youngquist, the president of Career Horizons, stated that 70-80% of jobs aren't even posted publicly. These under-the-radar roles go to friends, acquaintances, and referrals of people already working there or known to the HR department.

Those are truly powerful numbers. Yet many young people are reluctant to reach out and make the contacts that could result in job referrals. They might say, "That's not in my comfort zone. I don't like reaching out to people I don't know. Why should they help me?" or "I don't even like to ask people I *know* for help. I want to make it on my own."

Networking involves creating personal relationships. Most effective job searches involve making personal contact, finding someone who knows someone in the organization and asking for a connection, as well as going out and meeting people. But Millennials have grown up accustomed to connecting with the world via social media. This generation is less apt to use the phone for talking. Instead, many of them connect through texting. It's so easy, they say. Why would you call someone when you can text them? When it comes to networking, Millennials prefer to leverage job opportunities through the internet and social media.

And that's fine, as far as it goes. Many prospective employers encourage online job search—and job applications are located on company websites or recruiting sites. Often it's very difficult to even get through to a live person. But at some point, effective networking involves making personal contact, and that's where many young adults sometimes get stuck. They can rely so heavily on the internet that it becomes more comfortable and familiar to apply to an anonymous job posting than to reach out in person.

Why It's Hard to Reach Out

In my experience, Millennials are open-minded, conscientious, and eager to create success for themselves. But one of the college grads I coached shared with me her feeling that her generation is not used to making a great effort to overcome obstacles and really pursue the things they want. This makes sense when you think about the fact that the answer to almost every question can be found through Google, Siri, or Alexa. Information comes easily without the need to go to libraries or bookstores. Everything they want can be ordered online—they no longer need to leave the house to buy anything or talk to anyone, and therefore they miss the opportunity to interact and negotiate with people in the real world. Since just about everything is done online, many young college grads are missing out on opportunities to build rapport and trust, which are the foundation of any relationship. How can you, as a coach, help them gain the social skills and motivation they need to network?

Developing Confidence

Before grads can successfully negotiate the networking process, it is important to work through any limiting beliefs they might have. In general, when people don't believe in themselves, it erodes their confidence. While coaching young grads, I work through doubts and fears that may affect their ability to network.

I remind grads that networking is a little like dating. Today people are likely to meet online through dating apps rather than in person at bars and clubs. The skill of interacting and meeting people takes practice. I have coached many people—not just Millennials—who felt anxious about going out and meeting people. The thought makes them fearful, and the fear can prevent them from taking action. I help them refocus by having them set goals and intentions. We go over what they are going to say and do. What can they do to ease their mind so it becomes a fun, social experience to help them in their future? By working through their worries and apprehensions, they can see each situation as an opportunity to meet new people.

Networking is a form of sales. I usually get a less than positive reaction when I talk to young people about "selling themselves." That idea makes them feel anxious. To help them overcome this anxiety, I try to reframe the idea of "selling yourself" as simply having a conversation. Who you are, what skills you have, and what you are passionate about in life can be a good starting point. You are conversing with someone so they can to get to know you and the skills you have to offer, and to observe your social skills/behavior.

One challenge I have found in coaching members of this generation is their desire not to waste their time if it isn't going to bring them to the next step. I try to help them learn to be open to the next step in the process, even if that step is unclear.

Another challenge is negative thinking: If you believe networking is hard, then that will be your outcome. I suggest they switch to a new perspective and focus on whom they can meet and what can they learn from this experience. Then they will be open to all possibilities and usually have a better experience.

How to Make Networking Easier

How can job seekers embrace and improve the networking process?

1. Start with people they know. Personal contacts, or so-called "warm" leads, can be an easy resource to leverage. Coaches can suggest that Millennial clients make a list of everyone they know who might have a contact in their potential field, including their parents' friends and associates—even their family doctor! Most people are happy to help a young person get started. You never know who might turn out to be an important contact. Liam, whose quote began this chapter, so impressed his coach with his knowledge and creativity that the coach hired him to be social media strategist for her coaching company!

2. Help grads expand their list of contacts. They might have made assumptions that certain people are inaccessible. The basic skill of networking is being open-minded to the possibilities of what door will open. Who will lead them to an opportunity that can change their life? They won't know until they try.

3. Reach out to college contacts. It's easy to find alumni via LinkedIn who are working in the field in which they're searching. They should also contact the career counselor or advisor at their former college. These contacts are usually overlooked, yet they can be great for expanding their network. Millennials I've coached through the Grad Life Choices program have had success asking advisors and professors from their colleges for help. Many academics serve as consultants to companies and can open doors for their former students.

4. Seek out networking opportunities. In addition to going to job fairs, grads should check out professional associations that hold monthly meetings. These are usually open to those seeking to enter the field. Based on the individuals' career path, my clients and I discuss going online to look up job fairs and meet-up groups. I encourage them to talk to friends about their careers and ask for referrals to their friends and colleagues. Use LinkedIn to find new connections and ask existing ones for introductions.

5. Have an "elevator speech" ready. When meeting new people at a networking event or other get-togethers, job seekers need to be able to communicate who they are quickly and effectively. Having a prepared "elevator speech" is crucial. This is a short pitch lasting about 30 seconds (the time of an elevator ride) that describes who you are and why you are an excellent candidate for whatever position you are seeking. Have the grad practice the elevator speech with you. Here's a sample elevator speech that Liam might have used: "I've always been exceptionally passionate about music and theater.

I'm looking to work for a website that promotes the arts. While at college, I had primary responsibility for social media on the website Stage Buddy, which helps theatrical companies expand their markets. I'm fast, efficient, and have strong research skills. I think I would be an excellent fit for your website."

6. Use job board websites that list available positions to help guide and define the scope and direction of networking. Find as many job boards as possible, screening for jobs that interest you and for which you are qualified. This should include both the larger, commonly known sites like Monster, Indeed, and Job Monkey, and smaller sites focused on specific skill sets. Once you find a company with a job that interests you, check with your network to see if anyone has a connection to that company.

7. Set up informational interviews. One of the best and most overlooked tools in job searching is the informational interview, writes Jada A. Graves on U.S. News & World Report's website. An informational interview is a conversation with a professional who works in the grad's desired field or is employed by the company where he or she would like to work. The primary purpose is for the person to learn more about the industry or organization—it's not a job interview. But it can also be a great way to network. If the informational interview goes well, the person giving the interview might provide an inside track to current or future job openings.

What to say: Here's a way to open the conversation or what to put in an email or LinkedIn message. "I'm writing to you because my friend Sandy Klein thought you'd be a good person to talk to about getting into Human Resources. I know you have great experience in the field, and I would be very grateful to learn from your expertise and advice. I won't take more than 15 minutes of your time."

Getting an informational interview. For recent college grads, their school's alumni office should be a good source of names and contact information for alumni in the desired field. Grads should not be shy about approaching friends, family, and LinkedIn connections for contacts. Then the young person can send an email mentioning the contact's name and try to set up a meeting.

- Grads might also look up lists of members of professional associations and cold-call those working in nearby locations.
- Ask for a short meeting (say, 15 minutes) so the contacts know this won't disrupt their day.
- Plan 5-6 good questions in advance.
- Send a follow-up thank you note by email immediately after the meeting.

Preparing for a Networking Event, Job Fair, or Informational Interview

Millennials should:

- Have an updated, professional-looking resume. Bring multiple copies and carry them in a good-looking binder or case.
- Create business cards to leave with others.
- Look the part. Dress neatly in a professional-looking outfit or suit.
- Learn about the company and/or the industry they are applying to.
- Prepare questions for the person interviewing them as well as responses to questions they are likely to be asked.

Putting It All Together

Here's an example of how networking helped a young man in the Grad Life Choices program. Charles, 25, had been seeking a full-time permanent job in public relations, marketing, or communications for three years since graduation. He applied to dozens of positions on line and through recruiters, but all he got were temporary or contract jobs, which offered no health benefits and lasted only a few weeks or months. Charles took these jobs, of course, but he was always on the verge of not making his rent. He was at the end of his rope when he happened to mention to a friend that he had applied for a social media job at a major firm but, as usual, had heard nothing. The friend said, "I think my dad knows someone there, someone he commutes with on the New York bus." The friend's father asked for Charles's resume and sent it via LinkedIn to his commuting buddy, who was a senior VP at the company. Next thing Charles knew, he got called for an interview by the social media manager—and a month later he was hired for a full-time job. Charles had paved the way himself, taking the temp jobs, building his skills, creating a professional portfolio, and doing well at the interview. But the fortuitous bit of networking enabled him to get his foot in the door.

When college grads have belief in their skills, knowledge, and intelligence, they are more likely to seek out networking opportunities. They understand that the relationships they build can open a door in the future. Remind them that it is important to look up from the smartphone and computer screen and see who is around you. You never know; you could meet someone in Starbucks while reading this book!

Sandra Klein (Certified Professional Coach) was trained at iPEC (Institute for Professional Excellence in Coaching) and works as a partner and coach at Thought In Motion. Previously, Sandy worked in sales and marketing as district business manager at Schwarz Pharma, regional sales director at Inspire, sales executive at Roving Coach International, and Northeast district manager at Muro Pharmaceuticals. Sandy graduated from Northeastern University in Boston with a B.A. in languages. She lives in northern New Jersey.

CHAPTER 15

HOW TO LEVERAGE LINKEDIN AND OTHER SOCIAL MEDIA EFFECTIVELY

By Kim Pearlstein

> *"As a natural introvert, connecting with people is something I am constantly working on. I don't know a lot of professionals in my field. But by contacting friends of friends on LinkedIn, I've increased my network and even gotten some interviews."*
> —*KEVIN*

Years ago, the only way to look for a job was to search the "Help Wanted" section in the newspaper or go to a job fair. If you were lucky enough to know someone at a place you wanted to work or someone referred you, you might also land a job that way. In addition, it was more challenging to try to learn about the company you were interested in or the person who would be interviewing you.

It is hard to remember what the world was like before the internet. Advances in technology and the use of social media have transformed the way we communicate, learn, search for jobs, and promote a business. The job market continues to present many challenges, but today the availability of resources you can use to find a job is vast. In particular, social media and online tools, like LinkedIn, Monster, Dice, CareerBuilder, Indeed, and others have made it much easier to look for a job. Social media has continued to evolve over the years, and recruiters and employers are using it in full force. The job search landscape has become a two-way street, as recruiters and employers are now able to find you online if you are using social media and online tools effectively.

We may think that Millennials know everything they need to about the use of social media. This may be true of Facebook, Instagram and Twitter, but it is not true when it comes to the use of job-finding tools such as LinkedIn. A 2015 Pew Research Center study found that while 94% of recruiters and companies used LinkedIn for hiring, only 22% of 18-29-year-olds use it for job searches. While recognizing that it is most appropriate to have the client research the use of job-finding tools, it is important that the coach be sufficiently knowledgeable to guide the Millennials in the use of these instruments. This chapter describes the use of social media best practices and online job-finding tools. It's directed to Millennials and recent college grads, but coaches can use it to impart knowledge and strategies to their young clients. It is incumbent upon coaches to take the time to learn about social media and the online tools that can give their clients a competitive edge.

Job Search Strategies for Recent College Grads

You have access to more information than ever before, right at your fingertips, by using your computer or smartphone. You can search for and apply for jobs of interest by looking through online job boards, social media sites, and company websites and simply click a button to submit your resume. You can find job openings anywhere in the world, easily and instantly, as soon as positions are posted. There are upsides and downsides to using technology and the vast number of online resources available to search for jobs. Submitting resumes online is quick and easy with just the click of a button. But the abundance of online job postings can be overwhelming and hard to sort through. Many positions are posted in multiple places. For example, Indeed.com pulls from other job boards, as well as its own site, based on the criteria you enter. Also, different recruiting agencies might post the same job openings. Searching for jobs online all day and sending out a lot of resumes may feel productive but may get you nowhere. If this is the only activity you are doing, it is not enough. Getting away from your computer and building relationships by meeting people in person is also part of expanding your reach and finding opportunities.

In addition, it is a good idea to use the internet and social media to find information on potential employers. Finding company information is so easy today; you can learn a lot about the companies you are interested in so that you are better prepared for an interview. Review their company websites, as well as their LinkedIn, Facebook, and Twitter company pages and profiles of their employees, if available. Most exciting, though, is that social media has enabled you, as a job seeker, to be found by potential employers, hiring managers, and recruiters.

Tips to Get Started

Before starting your job search using social media, it is important to follow some basic guidelines. Remember that posting something on social media is putting it out there for anyone to see. Potential employers, as well as recruiters and hiring managers, are most likely reviewing the online profiles of job applicants in order to learn more about you. They want to "see" how you present yourself and determine what kind of person you are before they call you for an interview. As the saying goes, "You never get a second chance to make a first impression." Therefore, it is wise to follow these tips:

- Clean up your social media profiles (e.g., no photos of you drinking alcohol, no offensive comments). You do not want inappropriate photos or comments on your social profiles to negatively affect your ability to get a job.
- Have a consistent persona across all social media platforms.
- Complete all sections of your profiles. Having complete profiles on multiple platforms enables others to more easily find you for their job openings.
- Present yourself in a positive, memorable way.
- Make sure you adjust your privacy settings to control who sees what. On Facebook, you want to ensure that only your friends can see your content. On LinkedIn, however, you want your public profile to be visible to everyone.

Once you have "scrubbed" your existing social media profiles, but before you start searching for a job online, there are several important steps:

1. Create your story and "personal brand." Figure out your "Why" and make sure this information is included on your profiles, especially on LinkedIn in the Summary section.
2. Identify your ideal employers.
3. Identify some job goals and target industries for yourself. Ask yourself the following questions and write down your answers:
   - What are some key areas of work that I enjoy?
   - What are some work activities that I am good at or that others tell me I am good at?
   - What career and/or job titles am I targeting?
   - What specific industries or companies, if any, am I interested in?

Knowing the answers to these questions will help you target your job search to find the right opportunities that fit your goals. Remember to be professional and have consistency in how you present yourself across all social media profiles. Social media can enhance what you put on your resume, because it allows you to share what kind of person you are, what matters to you, and how you would be a good fit for a team and company culture.

The Best Ways to Use LinkedIn

LinkedIn is the best social media platform for finding employment opportunities, networking, doing research on potential future employers, and growing a business. Most likely, Millennials already have social media profiles set up on the main sites: Facebook, Instagram, Twitter, LinkedIn, and Pinterest. Of all the social media platforms available today, focusing your primary job search efforts on LinkedIn, instead of the other platforms, can help you land that interview. You might be thinking, "Why LinkedIn? Can't I just use Facebook and Twitter?" Here are several points worth noting:

- More than 94% of recruiters use LinkedIn to check out candidates, according to a Jobvite report in 2014. LinkedIn is the social platform most used by a company's upper management and human resources. A recent Society for Human Resource Management (SHRM) study found that 84% of organizations are now using social media to vet candidates.
- As of May 2017, LinkedIn had over 500 million members in over 200 countries and more than ten million active job listings providing users access to more than nine million companies worldwide. In the U.S. alone there were over 133 million users.

- When someone searches for your name on Google or other search engine, LinkedIn profiles often show up at the top of the search results.

According to Melonie Dodaro, author of *The LinkedIn Code*, "Getting a job today is not like it was five or even two years ago. Thankfully, a well-written LinkedIn profile is an invaluable resource when you are looking for a job. Not only can you actively use it to get an interview, it also helps recruiters and potential employers to find you." Since LinkedIn is the number one social media site to use to help you land a job, the rest of this chapter will focus on LinkedIn, with some mention of Twitter and Facebook.

Start with the Free Version: If you don't already have a LinkedIn account, simply go to www.linkedin.com to get started now with a free account. The free version of LinkedIn should suffice. I only recommend upgrading and paying for one of the premium LinkedIn accounts when you have hit a wall, where LinkedIn is restricting you from doing what you want, or you want more features. For example, the premium version of LinkedIn allows more search filters and searches, as well some additional tools (which LinkedIn is continually updating). You will probably be updating your profile on a regular basis, so it is essential to turn off your "Notifications." Once you land a job, before you add it to LinkedIn, turn the Notifications back on.

You can use LinkedIn to: establish your expertise, enhance your personal brand, grow your network, gain insight about the competition, find jobs and be found, find information about a company you are interviewing with, and more.

Essential Elements of an Optimized LinkedIn Profile
How would it feel to have recruiters and employers find you? LinkedIn is a search engine, like Google. Creating a professional,

employer-focused, achievement-based LinkedIn profile will help you stand out from the competition and enable you to be found more easily. There are key actions to take to "optimize" your profile so you can be found by recruiters, potential employers, and anyone else searching for a job title/role in your field or industry.

Optimizing your profile means putting the right keywords in the right places and completing all sections, as applicable. According to a LinkedIn study, you are 40% more likely to be found on LinkedIn if your profile is at or near 100% complete. Getting and keeping the attention of a recruiter or prospective employer is a key element in prompting them to reach out to you.

First, it is important to have a professional photo of yourself on your LinkedIn profile. Having a headshot photo on your profile makes it 14 times more likely to be viewed. Selfies do not convey this professional image. Some quick tips for a great photo: Smile with teeth, dress for your role, make eye contact with the camera, head to shoulders or head to waist in the frame. If you can't afford to hire a professional photographer, have a friend or family member take a photo of you, dressed professionally, against a white or solid color wall.

Next, research and identify the top three to five keywords that you would like to be found for, as you may have done when creating your resume. You can find keywords by reviewing recent job descriptions for the roles you are targeting and see what keywords are constantly repeated. Your LinkedIn profile should be consistent with what you say on your resume, in terms of your job experience, titles, timeframes, skills, education, etc. Add your identified keywords/keyword phrases to the following sections, at a minimum:

- Headline
- Summary
- Experience (job titles, current and past, as relevant)
- Skills

If there is a section I mention that you do not see on your profile, you can easily add it, when you are in "View Profile" mode. Look on the right side of the screen and click "Add new profile section." Choose to add a section by clicking the plus sign. Let's discuss the sections mentioned above in more detail.

Headline: This is the text directly below your name and offers you a way to stand out, as it is the first area people will see. You have 120 characters, so use them wisely; include your keywords and/or a compelling statement to capture attention and be memorable, in a positive way, of course. If you are looking for a job in Digital Marketing, your headline might read: Digital Marketing | Social Media | Branding. You could also use a phrase or statement, such as: "Help companies increase brand awareness with effective social media strategies." Another option would be to describe one fact you want people to know about you, what you are doing now and/or where you see yourself in the future. For example, you could state: "Customer service expert for luxury hotels." If you are challenged about what to say, you can get ideas from looking at the profiles of people you admire in your industry.

Summary: Share your story, be authentic, and let your unique personality shine through. Speak in the first person and describe yourself and your journey as if you were having a conversation. When someone is looking at your profile, only the first two lines of your Summary show up, until they choose "See more." You have up to 2,000 characters, but I recommend writing one or two short paragraphs (three to four sentences each), as well as including bullet points to highlight important skills and accomplishments. Include any special projects that you worked on in college and describe your achievements in terms that show how you solved a problem or challenge. Next, identify the types of positions you want and/or companies that you are looking to be part of. Add a "call to action" to make it easy for interested parties to reach out to you, such as:

"Connect with me on LinkedIn and contact me directly at [Email and/or phone number]."

Experience: Include your work history, with clear job titles (think keywords) and well-written job descriptions that highlight your responsibilities, as well as your key accomplishments and skills. Use bullet points to make it easier to read. You should not necessarily use the exact wording that is on your resume. Explain ways you have demonstrated success in a role or on a project or helped previous employers be more successful. How did you use your skills to produce results? Include specific contributions with metrics. For example, someone in the field of content marketing could say: "Used my writing and communication skills to develop valuable content for email newsletters, which increased email open rates by 10%." Include internships, part-time jobs, and summer jobs, as well as volunteer work. Volunteer positions show your character as someone who likes to give back. According to LinkedIn, one-fifth of hiring managers say they have hired someone because of their volunteer experience.

Skills and Education: You can list up to 50 skills on your profile. However, I recommend choosing at least 10 skills you excel at and want to be found for and add those first, in order of importance to you. You can always change the order later. Just as a compelling headline may do, including *relevant* skills may help influence recruiters and potential employers to take a deeper look at your profile. Simply start typing a skill name (e.g., Marketing, Public Relations, Customer Service), and either choose the skill from LinkedIn's list or create your own. Of course, don't forget to also include your education. In this section, add your school, degree, and major. Mention your skills and special projects, including any class assignments and extracurricular activities that demonstrate how you took a leadership role, achieved a goal, or overcame a challenge and what you learned.

Building Relationships

"Social media, at its core, is a communication channel like email or phone calls," states Jayson DeMers, Founder & CEO of AudienceBloom, a Seattle-based content marketing and social marketing agency. Interacting with people on social media can help you build relationships and establish yourself as a smart thinker in a particular area. Also, it is important to expand your network of connections, since the people you know can lead you to people they know, and thus you may find the right contact for landing your dream job.

Building online relationships is a good start, but make sure you take a break from your online job searching every once in a while and make in-person networking a part of your job search strategy. Once you have connected with someone online, schedule a phone call with them so you can learn more about each other. If they are local, set up an in-person meeting. Taking an online conversation offline will help build relationships with the people that could lead you to a lucky break.

Expanding Your Network of Connections

Grow your network by connecting with friends, family, classmates, professors, and previous employers/bosses. Use LinkedIn's Alumni feature to find others who attended the same school. These alumni could be potential mentors you can ask for advice or who may work at a company of interest to you. Strive to reach a minimum of 300 first-degree connections (people who are directly connected to you), as this expands your network enough to tap into the connections of your connections (what are considered your second-degree connections). Expanding your network of connections is extremely important, as the people who show up in search results are people who are your first-, second- or third-degree connections or those in the same group as you.

Always send a personalized connection request, and address the person by first name. For example, if you met someone at an event, follow up with a message like this: "Hi [first name], It was nice meeting you at the networking event in Morristown. Let's connect on LinkedIn to expand our networks. Have a great day! Regards, [your name]." To expand your network, it is fine to ask to connect with someone you don't know. With the free version of LinkedIn, you can send connection requests to second degree connections. Remember to personalize the connection request and state why you want to connect with the person. Your message could say something like: "Dear [first name], I am impressed with your LinkedIn profile (or background or company or achievements) and would like to connect with you here. Enjoy your day. Best, [your name]." In deciding whether to use their first or last name, ask yourself how you would address the individual if you met in person. I think it is a personal choice, based on your comfort level. (Make sure you actually look at their profile and are impressed with them, if you want to use this wording.) Remember to be yourself and write your message as if you were having a real conversation with that person.

Get Active: Some other activities that can prove valuable on LinkedIn are the following:

- Search for and join LinkedIn groups, both in your target industry and where you might find those who do the hiring. Ask questions, observe conversations, and "like" or comment on what people are sharing. **Note**: As of this writing, with the free version of LinkedIn, you can send up to 15 personal messages per month to group members, without being connected to them. This is a valuable way to reach out to key players in your industry or people who may be able to help you land a job.

- Post your own content (on your own home page and in groups) and share other people's content. This increases your online visibility and improves the chances of your profile being viewed by someone who can help you or might want to hire you.
- Get noticed by viewing the profiles of recruiters or potential employers, as you will show up on their "Who's viewed your profile" page.
- Get recommendations of your work from previous employers, professors, colleagues, or anyone who has overseen you in a volunteer capacity. These can add significant credibility to your profile and help you stand out from other candidates. Ask the person to state a key strength you demonstrated or a challenge you helped them overcome, and provide an example. (You don't want them to simply state that you were "a pleasure to work with.") **Note:** You must be directly connected to the person on LinkedIn in order to request a recommendation via LinkedIn. Go to the person's profile and click the three horizontal dots in the white box to the right of their profile photo. Click "Request a recommendation" and follow the prompts.

Be aware that there is also a LinkedIn App, which can be used to augment what you are doing from the LinkedIn website. However, there may be functional limitations of using the app, so most of your in-depth LinkedIn work (e.g., sending connection requests and doing research) should be done via the website.

Using Other Social Media

Although you can use LinkedIn as your primary social media platform to get interviews and find your dream job, remember that a potential employer will most likely look at several, if not all, of your social media profiles. Therefore, make sure you present yourself online in a consistent and professional manner. Let's take a moment to talk about Twitter and Facebook.

Twitter can be a valuable tool for learning from other professionals and leaders, as well as getting information on the industry you want to work in. If people are following you on Twitter, then it might be that you have something interesting or valuable to say. Interacting with like-minded people and building a community of followers online can show others that you are a thought leader, which could demonstrate that you are a great asset to a company.

Using **Facebook** can also be important. Actively engaging with others on Facebook may help you find job opportunities and can enhance your online visibility and name recognition. Some activities that are important are as follows:

- Find pages of businesses you want to follow and "Like" them.
- Post your own content, if relevant to the position you are seeking.
- Like and comment on other people's posts.
- Search and join local groups (e.g., Help Wanted groups, Business Forums, Small Business groups). You can look at which groups your connections are in to get ideas.

A final question to consider: When someone searches on LinkedIn or Google for what you do or want to do, will they find you or your competition? What will you do to make sure it is you? Take action today and get noticed online! To summarize:

- Be clear what you want, what you can contribute, and what differentiates you.

- Clean up and optimize your social media profiles, making sure to include the keywords for which you want to be found.
- Have a consistent message and "personal brand."
- Build relationships and expand your network.

You can build a powerful professional online presence to help you stand out from the competition and land your dream job!

Kim Pearlstein has a bachelor's in Accounting from the University of Delaware and a master's in management from New Jersey Institute of Technology. She is founder and CEO of Pearlmark LLC, which specializes in educating professionals on how to increase their visibility and grow their business by more effectively using email marketing (ConstantContact, LinkedIn, Facebook, and SendOutCards Greeting Cards). For more information about Kim's consulting practice, visit her website: www.pearlmarkvirtual.com. Also, feel free to send her a personalized LinkedIn connection request (www.linkedin.com/in/kimpearlstein) and tell her the best tip you learned from reading this chapter. Kim lives in New Jersey.

PART IV: FROM OBSTACLES TO OPPORTUNITIES

CHAPTER 16

BUMPS IN THE ROAD: COPING WITH FEARS, BLOCKS, AND GREMLINS

By Tenley Hardin

> *"There was always a 'but' when I first started talking with my coach. She made me realize that I was creating mental blocks, that I was imagining the worst possible scenarios. She taught me that I could do anything I want to do, that there are always ways around the 'buts.'"*
>
> *—EMMA*

A client once told me about a picture of her at age 5 wearing a pink tutu and a tiara. She says that every time she looks at that picture, she is reminded of the little girl who used to dance in her hallway and pretend she was a prima ballerina. She describes this young girl as whimsical, without a care in the world. This girl plays make-believe, talks to her pretend friends, and still believes in the tooth fairy and Santa Claus. She relies on the joy and love inside her to soothe her when she's scared. While she understands the difference between right and wrong, she hasn't yet learned the art of self-criticism. Her future has yet to be predicted, thought out, planned, or judged. She only knows that "the sun will come out tomorrow," a song from one of her favorite musicals, *Annie*.

Many of us can probably remember a time when we felt weightless, where nothing was holding us back. But then came the judgments, comparisons, criticisms, and expectations. We were told things that made us feel like we had to be something else, or we wouldn't fit in. Because we were young and impressionable, we actually believed the things people told us about ourselves, so much so that they became our narratives; subsequently, a tightly woven pattern in our brains began to develop, telling us that we'd always have to prove ourselves in order to be liked and accepted. And so we adapted and played along, because that's what everyone else did. Instead of imagining a world of possibilities, we saw limits and restrictions—things to box us in and make us look and act like everyone else. We yearned for individuality but found that it was often stifled as soon as we saw our peers eyeing us. We desired something more unique than the "everyday," but it got pushed aside for the sake of acceptance. And so we allowed negative thoughts to plague our minds. With each new experience and each new comparison, the thoughts increased, so much so that we developed fears, anxieties, and insecurities. In time, we created the Gremlin.

The Gremlin is the voice inside that tells us we're not enough. It tells us lies about our worthiness and points us in the direction of unhealthy thoughts and habits. Typically, we don't realize how harmful the Gremlin is until we are so frustrated by our current circumstances that we're not sure how to move forward. This is especially true for recent college graduates, who often feel lost, confused, and directionless. Such a lack of direction or clarity is only fueled by the Gremlin's haunting and toxic whispers: *Look around you. Everyone else seems to be doing fine, except you. You have no idea what you want to do. You're broke. You can't seem to figure your life out. Maybe you should just go take whatever job you can get. But then you'd be miserable. You're such a failure. You haven't done anything with your life or your degree yet.*

Think about how much even one negative thought debilitates your clients—how it stands in the way of their greatness. It is an energetic force blocking them from having that sense of weightlessness they may have felt when they were kids—when they never questioned whether they were "enough" to do anything. They explored. They searched. They questioned. They played. And all because such negative and critical thoughts hadn't quite nudged themselves into their brains just yet.

It's normal to judge ourselves, others, and/or our environments as a means to group, classify, and otherwise make sense of the world and people around us. However, when our judgments prevent us from accessing our truest potential and from moving forward in life, it is essential to confront and excavate what might be at the core of such judgments. If not confronted and dealt with, the Gremlin can control almost every aspect of our lives. Its constant nagging criticisms become our narratives. Since "we are what we think," in time, whatever the Gremlin tells us, we believe. And whatever we believe, we become. But what if instead of allowing the Gremlin to have such a tight grip on our thoughts, we learned how to confront it—disarm it even? Would we be afraid of what the Gremlin might truly tell us about ourselves? What would we see if we confronted the Gremlin? Pain? Shame? Guilt? What if we truly looked the Gremlin square in the eye and saw it for what it is: fear masquerading as criticism.

At the Core of the Gremlin Is Fear

Fear of succeeding. Fear of failing. Fear of losing acceptance from others. Fear of not being in control. Fear of becoming like someone they have a negative perception about. Fear that they don't have time. Fear that they have too much time and don't know what to do. With many of my older clients, such fears have been in place for quite some time. Fortunately for Millennials, that tightly woven pattern—like a braided rope—isn't as long; there's more flexibility there to pry it open and pull it apart. But in order to do that, they first need to examine where and when that rope was created.

When I first take my clients through the Gremlin process, I ensure that there's an established trust, as the Gremlin can get quite deep and a bit emotionally challenging at times. Usually by the second or third session, my clients have already expressed some of the negativities in their lives. As soon as they give me that opening where I feel like they've emotionally let me in, I go into the Gremlin process, because I believe it's the major block that stands in the way of their building a strong foundation for a successful and happy life. I ask them to tell me what the negative voice inside their heads says to them. Then, I explain who and what the Gremlin is—how at the core, the Gremlin is saying that they are not enough:

- *I just can't seem to get my life together*: "I am not organized enough."
- *Everyone else seems so successful*: "I am not capable or smart enough."
- *My parents are disappointed in how I've chosen to live*: "I am not a good enough child."
- *I have no idea what I'm good at*: "I am not talented enough."

One of my Millennial clients, Amanda, struggled with all four of these thoughts. Amanda attended a very well-known college on the East Coast. She majored in film and literature and moved to Brooklyn directly following graduation, hoping to find work in either advertising or media production. But after six months and only a few small jobs for independent film companies, she was not only broke but also incredibly deflated. She began waitressing to make money, but she hated going to the restaurant every day and dealing with customers. When she came to me, the negative thoughts in her head had consumed her life; her Gremlin was working overtime.

By session two, Amanda and I were knee-deep into her Gremlin, which we came to discover, first showed up in her life when she was in high school. Amanda's father used to demand to see her essays before she turned them in. Her father would sit at the kitchen table and go over every line with Amanda to ensure the essays were perfect, assuming he was helping Amanda develop into the writer she dreamed of one day becoming. But, in truth, this "editing process" was slowly stripping away Amanda's confidence and only making her more anxious about her abilities. She began to question whether or not she was a good writer—or if she even liked writing! As a kid Amanda would spend hours writing poetry in her room listening to her music, but as a high school student, she dreaded essay writing— so much so that she developed severe anxiety and was medicated as a result. When Amanda told me that she "had no idea what she was even good at," I immediately drew her back to this story, reminding her of the first time her Gremlin revealed itself—how it then only became even stronger and more deeply embedded as she allowed it to control her thoughts. This allowed Amanda an entrance into her fears of "not being talented enough."

I asked Amanda, "Why is it important for you to be talented enough? I mean, it must be, since you've allowed the Gremlin for years to tell you otherwise."

After some "I don't knows," she finally discovered the real fear: "When I was a kid, I was always told how talented I was. That sort of became how I was known. So if I am not talented enough, then what am I? Who am I? I am no one without talent. I am afraid of being someone without talent. I am afraid of being a no one."

I then asked her what it would look like to be a "no one with no talent."

"How would it feel?" I asked.

"Empty. Vacuous. Lifeless," she said.

I asked, "And how do you currently feel about your life?"

"Empty. Vacuous. Lifeless," she answered (Amanda drew this connection quite quickly; however, many of my clients still need a few more questions in order to arrive at this awareness).

"So, you've already created that narrative, haven't you? You've basically created an image of yourself that you feared the most," I said.

Amanda, like so many clients—and Millennials in particular—took what the Gremlin told her, believed it, and allowed it to seep into every crevice of her being (as illustrated by her anxiety). Subsequently, she embodied the exact thing she feared the most: being a no one. Essentially, she created her own reality, even though she despised the exact reality she was living! Once she was aware of this paradox, she was able to take responsibility for her reality, acknowledging that she has the power to create her own reality just by altering her thoughts. This awareness is necessary, because it encourages the client to move from a low level of energy (sadness, anxiety, guilt, shame, etc.) to a higher level of energy (responsibility), which prepares him or her for accessing even higher levels of energy.

Once Amanda took responsibility for her thoughts and her reality, I then guided her through a more thorough explanation of how our thoughts control our emotions, which inevitably control our outcomes. Here is the diagram I email my clients:

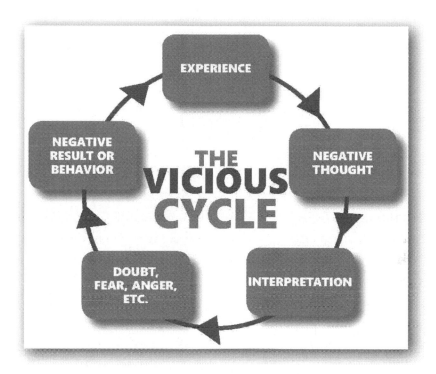

Notice in the diagram how the experience doesn't change, but our thoughts about it influence everything that follows. We can't always control the experience or outer circumstances; however, we can influence the outcomes. When we focus on changing *only* the emotion, we often judge ourselves for feeling a certain way. When we focus on changing *only* the behavior, we set unrealistic expectations for how we *should* act. And then when we don't follow through on a behavior, we judge ourselves even more harshly.

Initially, your clients may seem a little skeptical that by just changing their thoughts, they can change their outer circumstances. It's understandable, since those thoughts have been on autopilot for so long. I remind my clients who have the same concerns that it takes a lot of awareness and daily work to dismantle the negative thoughts and disarm the Gremlin. And even when we do—even then—the

Gremlin might return! But if we put in the work and are diligent about it, when the Gremlin returns, it gets easier to release its tight grip on our thoughts and emotions.

In order to help my clients begin to take control of their thoughts, I first assign them the "mission" of the Gremlin Letter. I typically assign this at the end of session 2 or 3 and allow them a week to complete it. The Gremlin Letter is their chance to let it all out—the good, the bad, the ugly, the in-between—everything! This exercise is perhaps one of the most powerful exercises I assign, because it not only helps my clients get very real with every negative thought they've ever said to themselves, but it also helps them feel more empowered to change their negative thought patterns.

The Gremlin Letter can be as long as your clients want it to be. Encourage your clients to be as open and honest as they possibly can, so that they can get the most out of this exercise. This is a pretty intense letter to write, so remind your clients that they should allow a good amount of time and privacy to be truly immersed in this exercise.

Along with the Gremlin Letter, I will email my clients the poem, "I Am Fear" by Lou Tice to help illustrate how fear can control us. I also include some questions about the poem:

- What emotions emerged for you while reading this poem?
- Do any of the lines resonate with you? If so, why?
- What lines do you agree with the most and why?

In that same email, I applaud them for being such courageous and soulful warriors, as they confront some of their deepest fears and most painful thoughts.

Please note: This exercise can get pretty emotional, so warn your clients that as they embark on this journey to self-love, they might first encounter some demons. Those demons are standing in the way of their happiness. Confronting the Gremlin in the letter can bring up some raw emotions, but in the end, such emotions are necessary to face, in order to release the Gremlin and access greater love, peace, joy, confidence, and fulfillment.

I Am Fear

I am Fear.
I am the menace that lurks in the paths of life, never visible to the eye but sharply felt in the heart.
I am the father of despair, the brother of procrastination, the enemy of progress, the tool of tyranny.
Born of ignorance and nursed on misguided thought, I have darkened more hopes, stifled more ambitions, shattered more ideals and prevented more accomplishments than history could record.
Like the changing chameleon, I assume many disguises.
I masquerade as caution.
I am sometimes known as doubt or worry.
But whatever I'm called, I am still fear, the obstacle of achievement.
I know no master but one; its name is Understanding.
I have no power but what the human mind gives me, and I vanish completely when the light of
Understanding reveals the facts as they really are, for I am really nothing.
—Lou Tice

Amanda's Gremlin Letter

Dear Gremlin,

Every time I hear your annoying and nagging voice, I feel like I can't do anything—like I'm a victim. You make me feel anxious and worried. You say things like "You're a failure.

You're directionless. You don't know what you want to do, because you're not focused or don't have any big talents. You have a four-year degree and nothing to show for it. You're going to be poor or end up with a job you hate." I hear your voice almost every day and I'm sick of it!

I remember you started up with your meanness when I was in high school. Right when I really thought that I was starting to be a good writer. But then you came along when my dad edited every paper I wrote and made me feel like a complete failure—like the worst writer ever. From then, I got anxious every time I had an essay due. I started to wonder if I even liked writing. In time, I even lost confidence when I would take tests, questioning my abilities. But then I got on Adderall and it made me feel like a superstar, though I knew deep down it was all superficial. That I was a phony. That it was the medication that made me smarter. It was like once the first negative thought came, a million more followed: *If I can't write, will I get into a good school? If I fail a test, then everyone will think I'm stupid. If I don't have my intelligence, then what am I? I'm not that pretty. Just average looking. I don't have a ton of friends, and I'm not an athlete. Just keep taking the pills, Mandy, and everything will work out.*

The pills worked for a while, until college when I stayed up for over two days and had to be hospitalized because I fainted. I was nauseous all the time. Bit my nails. Sure, on the outside, everyone thought I was this fun, happy, smart, and successful student. Fainting after studying for two days was par for the course. But they never knew the truth. They never knew that I skipped meals not because I was too busy, but because I loved the control of it. The fact that I could control something in my life when I felt so out of control. I'd call home and tell my parents I was fine. Was that your work too, Gremlin? You loved telling me lies about myself, so it seems you had no problem telling other people lies as well.

I am so ashamed that I listened to you. That I was so weak to believe your BS. I let you rule my life. I made some decisions that totally went against my values and were unhealthy. I made choices that didn't line up with what I truly want. Because of your judgment and negativity, I've hit a wall. I have no idea who I am anymore. I have kept this negativity hidden from almost everyone, until now, when I have no job, aside from waitressing, which I could've gotten without spending four years in college. I'm afraid to call my parents, afraid that they'll be even more disappointed in me. I'm sick of asking them for money.

All this negativity has made me so passive; nothing really gets me excited anymore. I feel like I've let time pass by, or worse let life pass me by. I had no idea you were this false voice, Gremlin! But the thing is, I realize all of this now. I realize I'm better than this. And you know what? I'm not going to let you do this to me anymore. I'm no longer a victim to your crazy need to feed off my low self-esteem, because really, I am inspiring, creative, and witty.

So, listen up, Gremlin! I'm no longer going to listen to you. Whenever you pop up—and I know you will because you're sneaky like that—I will first thank you for being there, because I realize you assume you're protecting me from taking risks. But after I thank you, I will immediately tell you to leave. Then, I will replace your voice with my own true voice and repeat positive thoughts. I want thoughts that make me feel important and special, so I can feel motivated to reach all the dreams and goals I have.

To continue my win over you for the rest of my life, I will repeat positive affirmations and intentions, until you're no longer an overpowering force in my life. The only force in my life will be the true voice of a girl who is happy, inspired, thankful, and motivated to help others. I am here to inspire people with my writing.

Farewell, Gremlin. Get ready for a good battle. Get ready to lose. The only winner is me: the real me.

Sincerely,

Amanda

After your clients shares their Gremlin Letter with you, always make sure to validate and affirm their thoughts, feelings, and experiences. You may then want to dig even further if necessary, helping them articulate their core fears aloud. Or, if you feel that their letter truly helped them understand all of their fears and how the Gremlin has controlled their life, then they are ready to break "The Vicious Cycle."

I first ask them:

1. Is the negative thought about _____ true?

Your clients might answer, "Yes" to this first question because a thought like, "I feel like everyone else has their life together, except me" could in fact *feel* true for them. But at the core of that thought is: "I'm not organized, smart, or capable enough." And is that really true? Can they know with 100% conviction that they are not organized, smart, or capable enough? Could they prove it 100% of the time? Probably not. This then allows them to realize the thought is an illusion. It's a lie their Gremlin has told them.

So, I then ask:

2. Where does the thought come from?

Often, the answer to this question is that the thought came from their experiences. Take them on a journey to that specific experience. Allow them to get in touch with the "story" they've been telling themselves for so many years. As such, they may gain a greater understanding of their own development—how and why they let such a thought pollute their minds. By facing the pain, hurt, anger, shame, and guilt that comes with such a thought, they are facing their Gremlin. They are not allowing the Gremlin to remain in the dark any longer. They are bringing it to the light just by talking about it with you. In doing so, they will be able to excavate the pain and release it. As they face the darkness, this is a prime moment to lend compassion and empathy. Validate and affirm all the pain and hurt the thoughts have brought them. Then...

3. Thank the thoughts/Gremlin for being there.

It may not feel like an opportunity for growth, but pain and darkness are there to help us grow. Our Gremlins are our greatest teachers. Help your clients feel the emotion behind the thoughts. Are they angry? If so, help them honor their anger. Are they lonely? Then have them thank the loneliness for being there to remind them that they're human, and as a human, they get to feel all the highs and lows of life. The point is to let them know that whatever they're feeling is okay. Encourage them to accept the insecurity and embrace the fear. It's all there to teach them a lesson about themselves. And then encourage them to constantly thank the Gremlin for being there. In doing so, they're not "at war" with the Gremlin. They're not in so much conflict with it. The Gremlin becomes disarmed, softening with their gratitude and acceptance of it. Finally, I ask:

4. How can you change the thought, so that it's more empowering and still feels real for you?

We don't just replace negative thoughts with positive thoughts. That wouldn't feel authentic. It's also not very healthy to just say, "I'm happy" or "All is well with me," when in fact we might be feeling pretty down about certain things in our lives. Instead, we break down the negative thought, examine the feeling, and then work on building a new and empowering thought that feels true for us. By asking them, "How can you change the thought, so that it's more empowering and still real for you?" you are guiding them to a new and empowering thought, but not glossing over the emotions they may still feel about the thought. For example, the thought, "I am organized, capable, and smart" might not feel "real" or authentic for them. What might feel better is, "While I may not be utilizing all my capabilities to their fullest potential, I know that I am capable enough to make my life work in positive ways."

After they learn this process, I will "assign" them the mission of applying this technique every single time they incur a negative thought about themselves:

1. Is the thought true?
2. Where is it coming from?
3. Thank the thought for its lesson.
4. What is a more empowering, but still authentic, thought?

Initially, it might feel a little tiring and somewhat robotic to examine every negative thought, since they are essentially reprogramming their brains and the stories they have created in their heads about themselves. But over time, breaking "The Vicious Cycle" will—like so many other habits—become second nature.

Once they make this "shift" and disarm the Gremlin, they create "The Empowering Cycle":

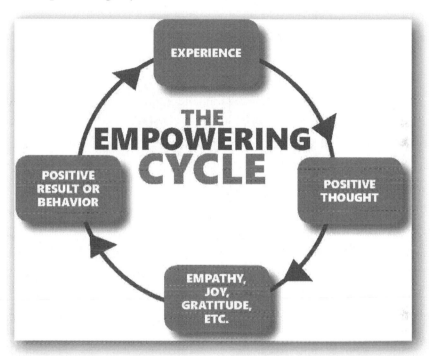

When your clients examine their Gremlins, break the "Vicious Cycle," create new thoughts, and build the "Empowering Cycle," they will feel more in control of who they are and what they want. This control will also generate more energy and motivation for them to make positive changes in their lives.

Like almost everything in our lives, disarming the Gremlin and creating the "Empowering Cycle" take time to develop as habits. As one of my clients said, "It's like building a muscle." However, such hard work is worth it, especially since our outer circumstances can often have a great effect on our thoughts and emotions. Having a solid method or strategy to rely on helps us feel more resilient when our outer circumstances aren't what we hoped they'd be. And more importantly, as we establish a deeper understanding and awareness of our Gremlin, we are then better equipped to not only face challenging times, but also create the reality we desire.

Tenley Hardin (Certified Professional Coach) was trained by iPEC (Institute for Professional Excellence in Coaching) and founded the coaching company Limitless Heart, which specializes in Intuition and Life Purpose coaching. Previously, Tenley taught high school and college English for eight years, and she has counseled high school and college students. She earned her B.A. from the University of Michigan and received a master's in Education from Belmont University. For more information about Tenley's coaching practice, visit her website at www.limitlessheart.com. Tenley lives in Los Angeles, CA.

CHAPTER 17

COACHING ACROSS CULTURAL DIFFERENCES

By Atina White

> *"I'm the first in my family to go to college,*
> *as we are Vietnamese refugees. Applying for*
> *and attending school brought many new challenges.*
> *I was very lost and chose a major without*
> *really knowing what it would entail.*
> *Haphazard as the choice was, I worked really*
> *hard and used every resource to graduate.*
> *It would mean a lot to me to see all that effort*
> *turn into something worthwhile."*
> *—LIEN*

More than ever, we live in a society characterized by diversity, and Millennials are leading the way. This generation is the most ethnically and racially diverse in U.S. history, with 44.2 percent part of a minority race or ethnic group, according to a 2015 U.S. Census Bureau report. Acknowledging and understanding cultural, ethnic, and even personality differences can have an important impact on the effective coaching of Millennials. This topic is of particular interest and importance to me as a woman who is African-American, Native American, and Swedish.

Growing up multiracial and bicultural with an African-American father and Swedish mother, I was not only exposed to those two cultures but also had the privilege of traveling to and living in Sweden, Spain, Kenya, and the U.S. As an adult, I've continued to be curious and passionate about understanding culture, receiving a Master of Arts in Intercultural Relations and incorporating cultural competence into my coaching practice. My cultural, ethnic, and educational backgrounds have influenced how I think, what I value, and how I interact with others. Knowing the impact my culture has on my own life, I anticipate that clients with different ethnicities, backgrounds, upbringings, and personalities also experience and approach life through their own unique lens.

Culture doesn't only mean country of origin, racial background, or socioeconomic class. It also includes the generation of which we're a part. For instance, the culture of Baby Boomers or Gen Xers is different from the culture of Millennials. The era in which Millennials have been raised—with social media, cell phones, and access to technology—is different from that of the generations before and can influence how they think, operate, and interact.

Why is it important in coaching to address differences? Each of us has our own unique background, which can influence our perspective and the way we coach. If we aren't aware of how this impacts others, we might not only miss out on providing effective coaching—we might even alienate our clients. I will share several examples from my own coaching experiences in which client culture, ethnicity, personality and/or background influenced our work. To do this, I will introduce two important cultural models (the Cultural Iceberg Model and the Bennett Developmental Model of Intercultural Sensitivity), identify some best practices, and provide examples of effective coaching across differences. The goal is to leave you with greater awareness, curiosity, and willingness to explore coaching across cultural and personality differences and to provide some tips you can apply with your own diverse Millennial clients.

The Cultural Iceberg Model: There's a Lot Below the Surface

When you envision an iceberg floating in the ocean, often all you see is a very small fraction of the entire iceberg. In fact, nine-tenths of an iceberg is out of sight or below the water line. Similarly, we consider nine-tenths of culture as out of our conscious awareness. Using myself as an example, the identity markers you can see are my gender, my clothing style, my age (roughly speaking), my body language, the food I eat, the art I display, and so on. Below the surface are many more aspects of my culture you cannot see or easily decipher. For example, values, beliefs, passions, tempo of work, preference for cooperation or competition, notions of modesty, concept of time, roles in relation to status by age, sex, class, occupation, kinship, etc. See chart of the Iceberg Concept of Culture below.

THE ICEBERG CONCEPT OF CULTURE

PRIMARILY IN AWARENESS

Fine arts   Literature

Drama   Classical music   Popular music

Dance   Games   Dress

Food   Language   Crafts   Celebrations

PRIMARILY OUT OF AWARENESS

Notions of modesty   Conception of beauty

Ideals governing child raising   Rules of descent   Cosmology

Relationship to animals   Patterns of superior/subordinate relations

Definition of sin   Courtship practices   Conception of justice   Incentives to work

Notions of leadership   Tempo of work   Patterns of group decision-making

Conception of cleanliness   Attitudes to the dependent   Theory of disease

Approaches to problem solving   Conception of status mobility   Eye behavior

Roles in relation to status by age, sex, class, occupation, kinship, etc.   Definition of insanity

Nature of friendship   Conception of "self"   Patterns of visual perception   Body language

Facial expressions   Notions about logic and validity   Patterns of handling emotions

Conversational patterns in various social contexts   Conception of past and future   Ordering of time

Preference for competition or cooperation   Social interaction rate   Notions of adolescence

Arrangement of physical space, etc.

Adapted from: AFS Orientation Handbook Vol. IV, 1984. © AFS Cultural Programs, Inc.

Here is an example of applying the cultural iceberg model in a coaching relationship. In 2015, I had the opportunity to coach Lien, a first-generation college graduate of Vietnamese descent. Her parents were Vietnamese refugees with minimal English language skills. In the introductory conversation to our coaching partnership, I introduced myself as a biracial and bicultural woman who had worked in higher education and was committed to making a difference for others. I shared that I grew up in New England and spent summers with my extended family in Sweden. I said that I came from a family that greatly valued education, hard work, respect, and social responsibility. I related my own struggle to find my passions, as my parents had high expectations and wanted me to pursue particular professions that weren't necessarily aligned with my interests and skills. I took the time to share these aspects of myself in the hopes that it might allow Lien the space to open up about *hidden* aspects of her identity as well. I did not ask her any direct questions about her background. I simply asked her if there was anything she wanted me to know. She chose not to share anything specific at that point.

However, throughout our time together Lien did open up about the challenges she faced because of her immigrant and cultural background. She struggled between choosing a job or career that would guarantee security and significant income but did not match her interests and values, or choosing to be a writer, painter, and/or creative artist, which wouldn't necessarily provide security or significant income but did align her interests and passions. Her parents' fears and reality of never having enough resources shaped a mindset for her to focus solely or at least mainly on making money. She was taught that success meant struggling, sacrificing, working extremely hard, and making as much money as you could.

By having an appreciation of our differing cultural backgrounds, we worked through various external as well as internalized challenges that were interrupting her pursuit of her personal interests and passions. Together we distinguished some limiting beliefs, acknowledged some cultural challenges, and identified actions she could take and careers she could explore that resonated with her. Neither of us wanted to dismiss her family and community values; however, we both wanted to focus on what worked best for Lien. Currently Lien is working as an account manager, a role that isn't exactly aligned with her interests and values. Yet she remains aware of and intent on ultimately finding a writing role in the arts, which could be both fulfilling and financially feasible for her.

Even if you as the coach do not share a cultural or ethnic background with your client, acknowledging and appreciating that difference can allow you both to move forward as partners.

To take "notions of modesty" as a concept of culture that is outside of our conscious awareness, here's another example of a conversation with a client. Joyce, a mixed-race Chinese-American woman, and I were discussing the practice of informational interviews in the job search process. I had introduced this approach several times before and noticed that Joyce was resistant and uncomfortable with the idea. After meeting professionals who had volunteered their time to speak with her, and offered to connect her with others, she still felt uncomfortable about taking them up on the offer. In a very non-coach-like way, I expressed the opinion that people in general enjoy helping others and she *shouldn't* feel awkward or uncomfortable making requests or accepting support.

As the conversation continued, I noticed her becoming increasingly distraught, and I felt a disconnect. At which point, with great credit to her courage and willingness to be vulnerable, Joyce reflected upon an aspect of her Chinese cultural upbringing. She had learned from her father, who had learned from his father, that modesty is important and asking for help outside your community is frowned upon. She proceeded to describe that in her culture modesty and humility are favored over accepting or asking for help or the support of strangers. She noted that this cultural context could be impacting her discomfort with networking and accepting support from people outside her Chinese-American community. It occurred to me that in educated, upper-class Caucasian-American culture, seeking support and assistance from others is accepted and encouraged. We both acknowledged the different perspectives, and I thanked her for addressing her frustration and naming part of her challenge with networking. We did not necessarily solve the challenge in that moment—yet being able to address it and have her concerns acknowledged allowed us to stay connected and in continued partnership. This cultural difference was important to address and acknowledge while not allowing it to hinder her exploratory process nor to create (or maintain) a disconnect between us.

When Joyce and I completed our work together, she shared how valuable the informational interviewing process had been in allowing her to gain greater clarity around her career pursuits. She also said that she was pleasantly surprised to learn how much people were willing to help her. I asked Joyce, "What in our conversation about Chinese culture made the difference for you to move forward with informational interviewing?" She said that having the opportunity to voice her discomfort, share her cultural perspective, and have that difference be acknowledged and accepted allowed her to step outside her comfort zone and explore something new.

Bennett Intercultural Sensitivity Model—From Denial to Integration

Bennett's Model of Intercultural Sensitivity is the second model I find extremely useful. This model explores the stages of cultural competence by which people learn to value and respond respectfully to people of all cultures (Bennett, M.J.,1993, in R.M. Paige *Education for the intercultural experience*. Yarmouth, M: Intercultural Press). Bennett asserts that as human beings we all can interact and interpret situations from different stages of cultural competence. We start with denial, defense, and minimization—known as stages of *ethnocentric thinking*. From there, as we become more aware, we can shift into acceptance, adaptation, and ultimately integration of other cultures—known as the *ethnorelative stages*. A chart of the Bennett Intercultural Sensitivity Model appears below.

BENNETT DEVELOPMENTAL MODEL OF
INTERCULTURAL
SENSITIVITY
Experience of difference

ETHNOCENTRIC STAGES	ETHNORELATIVE STAGES
Denial → Defense → Minimization	Acceptance → Adaptation → Integration

© Milton J. Bennett, 2017

An example of this concept is my experience as a college student. I studied abroad for a year in Sweden. As mentioned earlier, my mother's family is Swedish, and as a child I spent my summers playing with cousins on my grandmother's farm on the west coast of Sweden. So going to Sweden to study didn't so much seem like "studying abroad" so much as traveling to my second home. My first week in Stockholm, all the study abroad students were required to attend an orientation to learn more about Swedish culture and what to expect. At the time, coming from an ethnocentric mindset, I thought this was entirely unnecessary, as I already "knew" there was not much difference between American and Swedish people. It turns out I was operating in the stage of *denial*.

The program leader described aspects of Swedish culture that differ from American culture, which I felt were unimportant. For example, she noted that Swedish people are reserved, polite, and introverted. They can take a very long time to open up to a new person and are not quick to make new friends. However, once a friendship has been established it is deep and long-lasting. Another unique aspect to the Swedish culture she mentioned is represented by the word "lagom," which is loosely translated as "just the right amount" and speaks to a culture of moderation.

As the weeks went by I noticed myself getting defensive about American culture, as Swedes would tease me about my open and outgoing behavior. I found myself defending American thinking and feeling superior to some of my more reserved Swedish hallmates. Then I transitioned into minimization, where my peers and I began to notice there are differences between our cultures, yet we'd still minimize the significance of it.

Finally, as I continued to immerse myself in the community and attended social gatherings with Swedes and other international students from France, Spain, and Germany, we all began to accept and be interested in one another's cultural differences. I saw how we all enjoyed the different foods and daily life patterns. We appreciated the practical conveniences of Swedish life, such as the bus and train schedules that gave us the number of minutes until the next train on monitors above the tracks. By the end of my year in Stockholm, I'd become comfortable with aspects of my American culture that I was proud of and I had *integrated* aspects of the Swedish culture into my daily life.

For an entertaining look at the Bennett model in action, watch the film *The Hundred-Foot Journey*, the story of an Indian family that escapes turmoil in India and opens an Indian restaurant across the street from a world-famous French restaurant in France. The story humorously illustrates the stages of Bennett's model from denial to integration of cultural differences through the interactions and relationship between the French owner and the Indian family.

Applying the Cultural Models to Coaching

You may be wondering what all this has to do with coaching. I believe it has everything to do with coaching! If we deny, diminish, or ignore cultural differences between ourselves and our clients, we diminish our ability to connect, contribute, and collaborate with them. In the example I shared earlier about Joyce, if I denied or diminished her Chinese background, she might have remained disconnected from me, and lost trust in me. She might have shut down and perhaps even discontinued the coaching. But because we were able to accept the differences and work together to adapt and integrate her Chinese background into her job search activities, we remained connected and I believe we both learned and grew from the experience.

Another example occurred with Sara, a young African-American woman who was a first-generation college grad from the South. When we began our work together, I struggled to connect and engage with Sara. Her cultural background of Southern politeness and formality, in addition to her self-effacing, introverted, and quiet personality made it challenging for us to connect. As an outgoing Easterner, I made a false assumption that her quiet demeanor meant she was disengaged or disinterested. This could not have been further from the truth. Although Sara might have been introverted and cautious, she was a determined, hard-working, and motivated young woman. To improve our relationship, I began by offering to Skype instead of talk by phone so she was able to see me, which made her more comfortable. She appreciated and accepted this offer. In addition, I suggested that I email her some questions in advance of our calls, which she could either email back or answer during our calls. This gave her the chance to cover and add to any topic via email ahead of time and allowed us to have a specific agenda we could follow during our sessions. I learned that by adapting my coaching style to meet her needs we were able to create a successful partnership that, I trust, contributed to her landing a job in the field she was seeking.

As we coach Millennials and work to connect with their different cultural contexts in relation to achievement, work-life balance, job flexibility, and so on, it is so important to *accept* where they are coming from, work to *adapt* our coaching style to meet their needs, and *integrate* our increasing cultural awareness into our coaching interactions.

Building Cultural Competence

When it comes to cultural differences, avoidance or minimization often feels the most comfortable. Below are some simple practices that can contribute to cultural competence and to being effective coaches of our Millennial clients.

1. **Setting the foundation.** At the start of a coaching relationship, ask your client, "What do you want me to know about you?" or "Is there something I haven't asked that you would like to tell me?"

2. **Transparency.** It's okay to acknowledge if you are unfamiliar or unaware of something. Being open about my own lack of awareness and not hiding it when it shows up is critical.

3. **Share identity markers.** Let your client know some of the salient aspects of your identity, e.g., economic class, ethnicity, age, religion if relevant, values around culture and acceptance.

4. **Acknowledge the differences.** Explain your journey and how you think about race/culture/class dynamics.

5. **Be open to learning.** Come from a place of curiosity, not judgment.

6. **Don't assume.** Be conscious of where you make assumptions and be aware of where you might stereotype a group (i.e. gender, age, Asian-American)

7. **Check in with your client during and after the session.** Give clients choices as to how sessions are conducted to allow them to process information at their own pace. A question I ask my clients at the end of each session is "Was there anything missing, disempowering, or incomplete from our conversation today?" I want to give them an opportunity to share anything they may not have felt comfortable saying without a prompt.

8. **Be aware of cultural context—we're not authority figures, we're their partners**. Millennials may be accustomed to authorities telling them what to do. We want to remind them we are here to partner with them in identifying and obtaining employment that suits their skills and interests.

Becoming a culturally competent coach is an ongoing process. I invite you to take on the challenge and approach it with a keen sense of curiosity. Though I consider myself a culturally aware individual, I recognize there are always more aspects to a person's identity and personality below the surface. And there are always times where I notice my denial, defensiveness, or minimization of something different and work to accept, adapt, and integrate my new learnings as I did with Lien, Joyce, and Sara. Millennials are the most diverse, most interconnected, and most open generation to date. It's exciting to see what we can learn from them as we continue to deepen and expand our coaching capacities.

Atina White (Certified Professional Coach) has a B.A. from Brown University with honors in organizational behavior and management. Atina also earned a master's from Lesley University in intercultural relations. She received her coaching training at Accomplishment Coaching. Atina coaches individual clients through inquiry, support and guidance, and she designs and conducts group workshops and retreats. She was a Visiting Fellow in Programs and Development at Harvard University and program manager of the Social Enterprise Initiative at Harvard Business School. For more information about Atina's coaching practice, visit her website at: www.atinawhite.com. Atina lives in Boston, MA.

CHAPTER 18

FIRST IN THE FAMILY: COACHING FIRST-GENERATION COLLEGE GRADS

By Nicoletta Pichardo

> *"Toward the end of my college career all I wanted to do was get to the finish line. I just wanted the stress, testing, recording and experimenting to stop. I felt I wasn't doing as well as my classmates and I was worried about not having enough money even to feed myself."*
>
> —MARCO

Marco's Story

Marco grew up in a rough neighborhood of Camden, one of the poorest cities in New Jersey. While many of those around him succumbed to the hostile environment, Marco dreamed of great things. He would be the first in his family to go to college. He planned to become a doctor and return to help others in his city.

Marco's parents had immigrated from the Dominican Republic, and he was born in New Jersey. A bright and hard-working student, he excelled in middle school, won a scholarship to a private high school, and was accepted to an elite college in rural Pennsylvania on a partial scholarship, where he majored in biology. There he struggled.

As he explains it, "For the first time in my life I was alone and had to deal with an incredible work load without any support from my family or school. I had no money, and employment opportunities were few, especially without a car." Sometimes Marco couldn't afford to eat. Unlike his wealthier classmates, he couldn't afford to take unpaid internships to help him get ahead. He lost sight of his long-term vision and just wanted to get through school. He took an additional year to graduate.

After graduation, he moved back home and worried about paying off his student loans, which continued to accrue interest even while he was unemployed. Marco took the first job he could get, pushing carts at Home Depot for minimum wage and limited hours. Finally he found a job at the car auction where his sister worked, another detour from his original goals.

When I volunteered to coach Marco, he was grappling with the idea of reaching out for help. He was embarrassed to contact his network of classmates who had achieved career milestones when he hadn't. In addition, his family's needs were keeping him distracted from pursuing career opportunities.

Marco felt that he had lost the strength, optimism, and motivation that originally helped move him ahead. My coaching work with him was two-fold: to help him reconnect with this lost vision and passion—and to help him find meaningful employment that would move him toward his ultimate goals.

First-generation college students are an extremely rewarding group of young people to coach. They're aware of the fact that they want and need support. They've already proven they have a drive to succeed and are deeply grateful for the assistance they receive. It's helpful for coaches to be aware of the additional life challenges that these clients face.

Challenges in College

Going away to college is stressful for any young person. But for students who are the first in their family to seek higher education, the challenges are even greater. The academic and counseling support they had during high school often disappears. There are more independence and more responsibilities, but less structure and assistance in dealing with them.

In college they may have to work harder than students with more advantages, take time-consuming jobs to pay their way, and may be left feeling drained and exhausted—financially, emotionally, and physically. It's not surprising that 40% of students who drop out of college have parents who do not have a degree beyond high school, and 50% of those who drop out have a family income of $35,000 or less.

Despite the staggering odds, one-third of college students are the first in their families to enroll in higher education. But few of them graduate within six years, according to the Department of Education. Balancing school, work, and family without a robust support system causes many students to drop out, which almost happened to Marco.

And even if they do make it through college, first-generation grads face a variety of challenges that more well-to-do grads do not—they may have taken longer to get a degree, have overwhelming financial debt, and lack family support after graduation.

Challenges at Home

Most parents whose children are the first in the family to go to college are very proud and supportive of their kids. Many have sacrificed personally and financially to give them this opportunity. But being the first to attain a higher degree is not always looked upon favorably within the family. The grad might be branded as snobbish or not following community norms. There might be ambivalence toward the grad's achievements—high expectations of success but a lack of understanding for what it takes to reach these goals.

Lack of support from the family can come in a number of different forms. Young people might be expected to pay for the needs of their family and even extended family, rather than use income to pursue their career goals. There may be opposition for "stepping out," jeopardizing family bonds. Parents may expect attendance at all family events or want the grad to take care of younger children. They may not grasp the importance of the time their adult children need to spend studying for certifications or preparing for interviews when they could be doing paid work.

Lack of support and family demands can keep the grad from moving ahead. One of Marco's big fears was that after college he would be drawn back into the street life and family squabbles that he experienced when he was growing up. Helping Marco realize the powerful forces he was dealing with enabled him to recognize them as they were coming up, be better prepared to cope with these demands, and come up with ways to manage these additional stresses.

Cultural Challenges

The young person, having had exposure to a broader culture, is widening her horizons and creating new expectations. Success might be defined differently in the parent's culture—such as early marriage, having a child, or staying in the neighborhood. There may be a lack of acknowledgment for achievements or even a fear of leaving family traditions behind. For instance, Bavya, a young woman coached by Grad Life Choices, graduated from Indiana University with a goal of working in social media. She was unemployed and living with her traditional Indian parents, who were pressuring her to find a job they viewed as more suitable for a young woman from their culture. With the help of her coach, Bavya remained true to her own goals and found a job working for the website Angie's List.

Resource Issues

First-generation grads are impacted in several ways by their lack of funds. They often can't afford to pay for outside help, such as coaching, resume assistance, or therapy. In addition, they are likely to be saddled with debt, since college scholarships usually do not cover all costs. So grads might be left with student loans that are higher than the income of their parents. Increased stress and a sense of not being able to accomplish a goal are often a result. Malik graduated from the University of Louisville with $50,000 in student debt. He was behind in his payments and, to remove his negative credit rating, agreed to a schedule involving double payments for nine months. During this period he ate irregularly and imposed on various friends and relatives for lodging. He was able to sort all this out and ultimately find a job as project manager of a multicultural advertising agency with the help of his volunteer coach.

Working with Individual Needs

First-generation college grads can benefit greatly from coaching, but the demands on the coach may be different than with a typical client in some of the following ways:

- The coach acts as a type of anchor. He or she may be the only person who is dedicated on an ongoing basis to the achievement and success of the grad (without placing demands on the young person, as is typical in other relationships).

- The needs of young adults range from practical solutions ("Where do I go for help with my resume?" "How does networking work?" "How do I prepare for an interview?") to deeply reflective and personal areas ("What is my life's calling?" "How can I maintain this vision despite the challenges?").

- The coaching relationship may be more demanding than with other young adults, since their needs may be greater. The coach must remain vigilant of her coaching role as she may be also called on to act as counselor, mentor, friend, teacher, and advisor.

Tina's Story

One of the grads I coached, a young woman I'll call Tina, came from a large extended family. In her family, teenage pregnancy was the norm. Tina had suffered emotional abuse as a child, and her father left before she was 10 years old. Many members of her family had not finished high school, and most were on public assistance. Despite these hurdles, Tina did well in high school and got a job after graduation. Within a year, she realized that to live the life she wanted, she would need a college degree. She started at community college and continued to live at home to save money.

While classmates were able to enjoy their college experience, Tina lived in two worlds. At college she was absorbed in an environment of growth and study, with hope for something better in the future. At home she was drawn back into the dysfunctionality of her family.

After finishing community college, Tina was accepted into a four-year state university and managed not only to obtain her B.A.

but also to pursue her master's degree in social work. This was met with a lot of resistance from her family, who did not understand why she was spending so much of her time working on papers. They wanted her to attend large family gatherings and other events.

While in graduate school, Tina was able get a job in a residential mental health clinic on the night shift. But her income from work increased the financial demands the family placed on her. They felt that it was Tina's responsibility to pay for a disproportionate amount of the family spending. With the support of her coach, Tina was able to finish her MSW degree. She received a raise in pay and, just as important, was able to work normal daytime hours. Coaching also helped her address both guilt and anger she felt at herself and her family for the extra financial responsibilities that had been placed upon her.

8 Building Blocks for Success in Coaching First-Generation Grads

1. Plant the seeds

Creating the coaching relationship is always important with any client, but for this group of grads in particular, there may be much higher expectations and hope placed on the coach. A coach may find himself stretched in many directions—part coach, cheerleader, confidant, and mentor.

Establish clarity around your client's goal: Is it a job or career path? There may be dreams and long-term vision, but financial necessity may be driver for immediate job goals. Managing expectations of the coaching relationship, setting boundaries, and creating awareness around responsibilities of the client are all essential components of creating a supportive relationship right from the beginning. There may be a lot of chaos in the lives of these clients, and offering a structured, reliable relationship can serve as an anchor for them. Only then is it possible to plant the seed of possible future vision that allows the question to be asked: "What else is possible?"

2. Create space

Space for growth is a prerequisite for change to occur. Grads may want to work on their resume, for example, but not have a desk or computer. Creating space is about helping clients find systems that will support them in reaching their goals. Therefore, it's important to inquire about basic logistics: Is there a desk? Does the client have privacy and a private work area? How much time are they left with after all of their family responsibilities? Transportation can be an issue. They may not have a car and must rely on public transportation to get to interviews. What about access to computer/internet—at home, at school, or at the library? If they have a shift job, personal time and fatigue could become issues. It is important for the coach to realize that it may be difficult for grads to maintain privacy during the coaching call if they are sharing a bedroom (or may not have a phone of their own).

3. Design the path

Visioning: Many young people are frustrated and discouraged because they have lost momentum on their original goal, or it may be clear to them that they will not be able to reach their original goal. There may be feelings not only of frustration and discouragement but also anger at themselves. Visioning can help them overcome these feelings and move forward.

Instead of asking clients what they want to do with their life, I ask them to get internally still and quiet. Then I ask a series of questions, and we explore what visions come to them. In Marco's case, I asked him where he envisioned himself in six months? One year? Five years? In each case he came up with a career path leading into the medical field.

4. Set up systems for success.

Young people often need help building the scaffolding or structure for their job search. Help the grad figure out spaces for networking, such as professional clubs and associations, and whom they can call on for help (e.g., college counseling center, LinkedIn, professional network).

At times they need you to be a mentor—sharing your experiences, expectations, and things that have helped. They may also need practical solutions: How do I do networking? What do I wear to an interview?

Fears are not unusual for any new grad, but more so for first-generation grads: fear of interviewing, fear of becoming a professional, fear of disappointment if don't get the job, fear of disappointing others who have helped in the past. Reassure them that they can prepare for whatever it is that is creating their fear by breaking a large issue into small steps.

Some common issues that coaches need to be aware of with first-generation clients include:

- Blaming: The feeling that "kids from other families have it easier, I wasn't aware that such-and-such even existed..." Marco told me: "I didn't know I couldn't wear a sports outfit from gym to a job interview. It wasn't my fault."
- Distractions: Recognize that some things deserve our utmost attention, others don't. It's important for grads to learn to differentiate or they will not reach their goals.

- Prioritizing: Figuring out what needs to be done first, what can wait for later. Learning to set new priorities in order to reach new milestones can be a challenge.

5. Create a "balance sheet"

The goal is to recognize all the things that *are* working for them, helping them to keep their balance. Your clients may only come up with a few things and say, "That's it." Challenge them to keep going for as long as possible. (This would be a good homework assignment between sessions.) Have the grad start brainstorming ALL of their assets (language skills, housing repairs, ability to get around, ability to problem-solve, previous achievements large and small, etc.). The goal is to recognize that, in spite of challenges, clients have a lot going for them that they can build upon. This list can be used throughout coaching sessions to draw upon available strengths/resources to overcome challenges.

6. Affirmations

End each coaching session with two affirmations: one from the coach for the client, and one affirmation that the client can say about him/herself. This helps shift the client's focus away from negativity and helps build the coaching relationship, as clients often do not have sources other than the coach for recognition/affirmation.

7. Results-focused thinking

When reviewing action items, focus on the results the client will have rather than focusing on simply completing the activity. This involves making a connection between the goal and what makes this goal important: "Why do I want to reach this?" This technique is very helpful in shifting someone from being busy all the time to engaging in meaningful activities that are results driven, thereby creating less stress. The client will learn to ask himself, "What is the result of this activity?" prior to doing an activity. For instance, when writing an email to get a recommendation, the client will ask himself, "What is the result of *this* email?" Once he has clarity about the goal, he can check to see all the necessary information and questions are included.

8. Breaking it down

Help the client realize the significance of small steps in reaching big goals. Often clients only see the large goal (i.e., the dream job—preferably right now). What can be done today to meet this long-term goal?

This involves REALLY breaking things down to smallest parts (e.g., making an appointment with someone, following up an interview with a thank-you note in a specified amount of time, helping client outline every single step in reaching goal—often necessary steps are unclear to client).

Marco's Story, Continued: A Positive Outcome

About two months into our coaching, Marco emailed me the great news that he had been hired as a technician in a blood lab. He had done very well on a series of interviews with three people, and the next day the HR manager reached out to him with a job offer. "I am very excited to begin this new chapter in my life," he wrote. "I am especially happy about this opportunity because this time I will truly be making a difference in the capacity that I have hoped for."

A month later, Marco sent an update. "Everything is going very well. I'm thankful to be working again, especially in the medical field. I am still in training for now. There is much to learn and relearn, since I am a bit out of practice. But I'm still confident that I can do a good job.

"I can't thank you enough for all your advice and suggestions," he continued. "You truly put me in touch with the inner motivation I thought I had lost a long time ago. I will never forget all that you have done for me, which goes beyond just phone conversations. I hope to hear from you in the future and thank you for all that you do for people like myself."

For a coach, there is no greater reward. I wrote back, "I'm truly excited and happy about the direction your life is taking. It sounds like things are moving forward just as you envisioned—the result of your dedication and hard work!" It was my privilege to work with Marco, and I let him know that although our work had come to a close for now, I would continue to be a resource for him to draw on in the future.

I have found that most first-generation grads really do know what they want—but they may have gotten lost along the way after college. As a coach, I try to offer the support and guidance so the grad can once again see their path, reconnect with their vision, and move toward their long-term goal. Coaching first-generation college grads can be the most satisfying of coaching experiences. Knowing that a pioneering young person is continuing the journey towards his or her vision as a result of coaching is both a humbling and incredibly rewarding experience for a coach.

Nicoletta Pichardo (Certified Professional Coach) has a B.A. degree in psychology and a master's in education (concentration in counseling), both earned at the University of Texas. She received her coach training at iPEC (Institute for Professional Excellence in Coaching). Nicoletta has her own coaching company (Navigo Coaching). As a Professional Life Transition Coach, she is driven to help clients step out of stress, overwhelm, and limits by unlocking and unblocking what is holding them back. She has held leadership roles in international organizations and nonprofit boards of directors. A native of Munich Germany, Nicoletta calls Washington, D.C. her home.

CHAPTER 19

HELPING GRADS DEAL WITH STUDENT DEBT

By Ellen Reichert

> *"I have a law degree, am saddled with over $100,000 in education loans, and I can't find a decent law job. I'd like to consider a change in fields to web development (I once worked at that and liked it very much) but may be trapped by my debt."*
> —MARK

As you may already have read, Millennials are now the largest generation and they differ in many ways from the generations that came before. One of the differences is that they are on track to be the most educated of all previous generations, with one-quarter finishing at least a bachelor's degree, compared with 19% of Gen Xers and 14% of Boomers, according to a 2015 Pew Research study. But college and advanced degree costs have continued to rise, and as a result Millennials face significant student loan debt unparalleled by earlier generations.

To put this in perspective, an online Wall Street Journal article noted in 2015 that "Millennials and debt go hand-in-hand." Citing research done by National Financial Capability Study, the WSJ found that "two-thirds of Millennials have at least one source of long-term debt outstanding—whether student loans, home mortgages or car payments—and 30% have more than one. Among the college-edu-cated, a staggering 81% have at least one source of long-term debt." In addition to long-term debt, they also carry short-term debt from credit cards. In fact, an article in Forbes online by Maggie McGrath stated that 30% of Millennials said they would even sell an organ to get rid of student debt!

The burden of debt creates other challenges for this generation. Among these are:

- Worries about being able to pay back their loans
- Living at home with parents longer
- Putting off marriage longer
- Delays in purchasing a home or car

If you are coaching a Millennial, it's important to recognize that debt may be a part of your client's life and may have an impact on the achievement of their personal goals. Reframing your understanding and setting aside your own beliefs about debt in order to help your clients achieve their financial goals is imperative in order for you to help them. Leave your own thoughts on debt and any judgment you might have at the door and *accept what is* for your client. From the safe space you create, your client can create a plan and develop solutions to move forward.

A recent law school graduate with whom I worked needed additional money to support himself while studying for the bar exam. In addition to his part-time job, he sold personal items and collectibles on eBay in order to make ends meet. His biggest concern after he passes the bar is finding a position that will allow him to begin to pay back his loans and afford to live on his own.

Another recent college graduate decided to move in with his girl-friend after graduation. This couple were very focused on reducing their cost of living. They looked for an affordable place a short distance from their jobs. They furnished their apartment by asking friends and neighbors of their parents if they had any items they were looking to get rid of. Without spending money on anything other than a mattress, they were able to furnish their home while helping their families' friends and neighbors get rid of unwanted or no longer used furniture.

7 Steps to Help Grads Manage College Debt

The financial challenges for the Millennials are real, and as coaches we have several ways of helping our clients make positive progress toward achieving their goals and getting on a better financial footing. And you don't need to be a financial advisor to do it.

1. Define the Current Situation

Help your clients to define where they are today. What are their current financial challenges? What are they most concerned about? To make positive steps toward their financial goals and to realize their personal dreams, it's important to know where they are now so you can help them to build from there. Think of it as an accounting ledger. Your client needs to know what is coming in and what is going out, and any debt, interest charges or fees fall into the expense side of the ledger.

Exercise: Ask your client to make a simple ledger. Place two columns on a page. In the first column, list all of the income or revenue they are receiving. (Money from Mom and Dad is income, but if your clients are trying to live on their own, ask them to leave that out for now.) Then, in the second column, have them list all of their expenses by line item. This is important because if your clients have a credit card, they may see that as a single line item. If so, ask them to break it down so they can see where their credit card purchases are actually spent. Millennials tend to use debit or credit cards for payment rather than cash, so really looking at where their money is spent is key to being able to reduce or eliminate expenses.

2. Clarify the Desired Situation

Once your clients have developed their view of their current revenue vs. expenses, then you can co-create the desired state. Knowing the revenue side of the equation will enable your clients to make strategic choices about their expenses and how they want to move forward. What is needed to live on? What are they saving toward? What debt needs to be paid? What is the time horizon for paying back any outstanding debt or loans? Where can they reduce expenses? How could they find creative ways to reduce their expenses or increase their revenue?

Tips: Your client might be able to barter for services with someone who provides what he needs and offer his services in return. Using alternative forms of transportation may cut down on expenses. Shopping at thrift stores or resale shops is a great way to find never-worn or well-cared-for clothes, often with designer labels, at much less than you would pay off the rack at a department store or boutique. Even apps like ShopSavvy can help find a product at the best price in your area. Brainstorm: How can you get what you need for less? What resources are out there to find great deals?

3. Identify Specific Goals

Help your clients figure out their goals. What do they want to do with their money? What are their immediate goals and what are their longer-term goals? Ask them to be specific. Think about the future: Where do they want to be in 10 years? Describe it. What does it look like? What will their ledger look like then?

4. Establish Priorities

With their goals spelled out in detail, it's time to establish their priorities. This might require some finesse and balance, some trade-offs or compromises. Expect some back and forth here before settling on a list of priorities. Your ability as a coach to reflect back what you hear will help your clients to see contradictions in their thinking; for instance, when then they say they want to pay off their debt while making the purchase of an expensive home as number one on their list of priorities. Assuming that managing their debt is a priority, you have an opportunity to remind them of their goals and help them find the possibility of realizing their dreams over time.

5. Put First Things First

Be sure you and your client are absolutely clear on what *is* the client's top priority and revisit it often to be clear on the agreement or restate it. It could be finding a better paying job to better enable paying off student loans. Or it might be setting up an automatic payment schedule to pay down debt. Or it might be doing the minimum payment on their loans now so that they can realize their goal of living on their own. Whatever it is, make a point to bring the client back to what you agreed on as the top priority. With each subsequent goal, be clear as to how it contributes or detracts from goals with higher priority. The ordering of priorities should not be written in stone, however. As your client's thinking clarifies, it may be necessary to explore whether the order of priorities needs to change.

6. Prepare a Realistic Budget

It wouldn't be a financial plan without a budget! Helping your client to establish a way to achieve their financial goals is extremely valuable. It's the rule of "what gets measured, gets done" in action.

Tip: There are so many fabulous tools these days that make it easy to track expenses, including Mint and You Need a Budget—even an old-fashioned Excel spreadsheet will do. Your client's bank may even have an online tool. For Millennials, apps seem to work best, so challenge them to find one that works best for them.

7. Develop a Timeline

When it comes to moving beyond debt or achieving goals, it's important to have a time horizon. They should know how much time it will take to get to where they want to be. The best approach is a formula that takes into account the length of the loan, and what they want to pay each month to get there. Remember: Student loans are often much different than traditional car or mortgage loans. Be sure your client is totally aware of the details of their loan and what is required to repay it.

8. Make Commitments and Take Action

Ask your client to commit to the actions they have defined to move forward toward their priority and their goals. Ask them how they will measure their success. Challenge them to look at their budget and see what they can adjust to make their goals more attainable or achieve them in a shorter time frame. Hold them accountable to the actions they have committed to take.

Debt Is Manageable!

Like anything else in life, we can help our clients determine what outcome they want to achieve and support them in creating a proactive plan to get there. Then they can see that by breaking it down into manageable steps they can achieve it! If we can help them focus on what *is* possible and in their control, they will realize positive movement going forward.

Ellen Reichert (Professional Certified Coach) has a B.A. degree in communications from the University of Missouri and received her coaching education from Coach University. She is the founder of Whiteboard Coaching, LLC., and is a business coach for Edward Jones Company. In addition to coaching, Ellen's career has focused on marketing and employee engagement. She has been manager and director of Solution Design for O.C. Tanner, Staples, and Corporate Express, and has held various positions in advertising. Ellen lives in the St. Louis area.

CHAPTER 20

THE CHALLENGES OF MOVING BACK HOME

By Amy Alpert

> *"I am currently coming up on the end of my one-year paid*
> *internship that makes me very little money, and I haven't*
> *been able to pay on my student loan, which is a real concern.*
> *At the end of this month, it looks like my only option is*
> *to move home until I figure out what I can do next."*
> —CHLOE

Returning home after college is a bit of a culture shock, to say the least. After four years of independence, a young adult must recalibrate his or her roles and relationships with family. On top of that, graduates are trying to make the adjustment from a student identity to life as an employee or job seeker. With all of these changes, coaches have an opportunity to help their clients navigate these new roles and responsibilities.

Today moving home after college is the norm. According to a 2016 Pew Research study, "Living with a parent is the most common living arrangement for young adults for the first time on record." With increasing student loan debt and a challenging job market, it is difficult for graduates to embark on their own immediately. Returning home can provide the necessary cushion to focus on a job search full-time or to limit expenses while starting out in an entry-level job.

The keys to success with moving home are to develop an exit strategy while seeking opportunities for growth in the interim. As one young adult told me with a chuckle, "I thought of my time at home as like jail—but in a good way." Extreme? Perhaps. Of course, the individual above also talked about his gratitude to his parents and the way in which his time at home helped him. However, a dual perspective is a useful way for young adults to approach time at home with a realistic attitude: Don't get too comfortable, but do make the most of the present circumstances.

Young people face many challenges when returning to the nest. The following are some of the ways in which coaches can help their young clients resolve these challenges and move ahead as independent adults.

Creating Structure

One of the first things unemployed grads need when they move back home is structure. Without the ready-made framework and feedback provided by classes or a job, young people can easily become disorganized and unmotivated. A coach can be very helpful in pointing out the need for structure and helping the grad create a schedule. Job seekers need to plan out their day, ensuring they wake up at a certain time, do productive work, and also have opportunities to pursue hobbies and socialize. Helping around the house should also be scheduled into the day.

Creating a schedule can be challenging for new grads. First, they have not been living by a standard daytime work schedule (for instance, students might have classes only in the afternoon or stay up all night writing papers). Second, job seeking requires a lot of self-direction and drive. Finally, there may be competing activities that can throw young adults off track. For instance, one of my clients was suffering from insomnia, which was very detrimental to her ability to be productive. When I asked more questions about her schedule, she revealed to me that her father worked the night shift, so she would often stay up to see him. While this was a great way for her to bond with her father, it was interfering with her ability create a workable schedule for herself. Together we figured out a plan to help her work around this obstacle.

I interviewed one very motivated individual, David, who was seeking a career in the highly competitive field of filmmaking. He decided to take a job at a local movie theater so that he was not "sitting around all the time." He did this for himself but also for his parents, since it was hard for them to see him at home so much. In the end, working at a movie theater had its perks and benefits. David was able to see films as soon as they were released, which for a future filmmaker meant a lot. He was able to create a schedule for job seeking around his part-time job, which provided structure. Plus, his parents were happy he was making some money. Flexibility, hard work, and creativity can provide lots of ways to build a workable schedule for these grads. Looking at time differently with the help of a coach is essential to the transition from college to "real life."

Staying on Track

Helping grads uncover their goal is another way coaches can help. By clarifying steps towards that goal, a coach can provide accountability at a time when a young adult's motivation might be low.

Young people often appreciate having someone to keep them on track, and it is usually best if this person is not their parent. By identifying tasks to complete between coaching sessions, grads can figure out how to work these responsibilities into their daily schedule. Then, at the sessions, they can report back to the coach on what they've achieved. Sometimes it is helpful to have clients submit an agenda before meetings to help them think through what they need to accomplish and what they want to focus on. Giving them a sense of supported autonomy is a beneficial way to help them to maneuver towards their goals and ultimately function completely independently.

Lisa, a Millennial who was living at home in Indianapolis, had a goal of finding a job in New York City. Her coach not only encouraged her to take a trip to New York to explore opportunities, but she helped Lisa plan out the trip so it was as productive as possible. Lisa set up several networking meetings for her visit, pushing herself to contact friends of friends. She ended up finding a job in New York as a result of one of these meetings and was able to move out of her parents' home within months. In this instance, a coach not only gave her the confidence to pursue her dream of moving to New York, but also helped her develop the practical skills to best utilize her visit to make this dream a reality.

Sharing in Family Responsibilities

"Being in college is not real life," said one of my clients. College can be like living in a bubble, so coming home can provide a gentle transition to adult life. Taking on responsibilities at home is essential. A grad can and should participate in tasks like grocery shopping, cleaning a house, paying bills, caring for a lawn, and basic home maintenance.

David, the grad I mentioned above, explained to me that when he moved home with his parents they divided the family responsibilities three ways. He was now an equal contributing member to the home. Since one of his goals was to have a positive relationship with his parents during this potentially stressful time, the more David contributed, the better for everyone.

While David's family had an informal understanding about the new division of labor, it is a good idea for families to communicate in a very clear way about new expectations. Coaches can help clients communicate with parents. Some families go so far as to create contracts together so that everything is very clear. In any case, the more grads participate in the home, the better prepared they are for adult life and the better parents feel about having their grownup child back home.

In some cases, adult children (if they are working) are asked to pay a nominal rent or share in family expenses. Asking kids to pay rent is a subject of some debate. A lot depends on the individual family situation: If the grad is financially strapped and paying back student loans, this rent-free time is a blessing. But if the grad is spending a lot of money on going out with friends, parents might understandably resent being asked to foot the bill for everything else. In some cases, if they can afford it, parents hold onto the rent money and present it back to their children when they move into their own place. Again, a coach can help a young client think through what will enhance the family relationship and the grad's independence.

Creating an Exit Strategy

An exit strategy can be highly motivating for young adults. One Millennial I spoke with, Steve, decided to take on an additional part-time job in order to expedite the opportunity to move out of his parents' house. He realized that he would not be able to move out on his timetable with the income he currently had, so he found a part-time job that allowed him to pull in more money and move out sooner. Steve decided to continue working multiple jobs when he moved out to keep building his savings. Living at home and creating an exit strategy lit a fire under him and helped him develop a very strong work ethic going forward.

An exit strategy can also be a helpful way to bolster the parent-child relationship. Parents can feel overwhelmed with their children returning home and fear "the worst"—that their kids will never venture out on their own. Establishing an exit strategy can reassure parents that this is a temporary arrangement. An exit strategy can also help with the opposite scenario. One young woman I spoke with felt that her mother was a little too thrilled that she had moved back home. The grad felt pressure to fill her mother's emotional needs. So an exit strategy can also be a reality check for parents who are eager to have their nest filled again.

Pursuing Opportunities for Growth

Having the cushion of living at home can allow for opportunities for growth outside of looking for a new job. Having shelter provided can give young people a bit of freedom to develop other parts of themselves—not just what is necessary for a career.

John, a grad I interviewed, gave stand-up comedy and competitive boxing a try while living at home and job hunting after college. His coach encouraged him to take risks and stretch beyond his comfort zone. Neither experience resulted in a job in and of itself, but he now credits his time doing stand-up and boxing as the reason he can handle work presentations without breaking a sweat. John also looks back on that time of his life fondly. He feels he did not squander his time at home—rather he took the opportunity to try some things he might never have had the chance to do otherwise.

Will, a 23-year-old who had majored in English, moved back home after college with no clear idea of what job he could do. He held a number of temporary positions, but none were interesting to him or provided any kind of career path. At his coach's suggestion, Will interviewed friends in a variety of fields, and one of them was highly enthusiastic about his work in IT for a startup. "If you have programming skills, you can get a job anywhere," his friend said. Will took a free online course and discovered to his surprise that he found it fascinating. He started a certification program in coding and committed to spending three hours a day on his courses and assignments. Had Will not lived at home without an immediate need for money, he might not have had that opportunity to pursue an interest that he hopes will turn into a real career.

Creating an Adult Relationship with Parents

One of the best ways for grads to make the most of their time at home is to work on developing a more mature relationship with their parents. This can be challenging, as young people find themselves once again in a dependent position in their childhood home. For instance, grads and their parents have to negotiate new approaches to privacy and advice-giving that don't feel intrusive. As one mother of a returning young adult wrote on the website Next Avenue, "It's hard not to ask what to me seems the most natural (and polite) of questions: 'Where are you headed?'"

But working on an adult relationship is an effort worth encouraging. As one Millennial, Craig, insightfully revealed to me, his time at home forced him to deal with some deeper issues in his relationship with his parents. He might never have uncovered and dealt with these issues had he not moved back home after college. By working on their relationship as adults, Craig feels closer to his parents than ever. He realizes that had he not had this time with his parents, he might have been content with a superficial relationship with them rather than the deeper and more authentic relationship they have developed.

Another Millennial I spoke with encouraged his dad to start biking, and they would bike together while he lived at home. Both father and son benefited from this healthy habit and the time together. Coaches can encourage their clients to find ways to connect with their parents in new ways, which not only can improve their current relationship but also benefit them for years to come.

Providing Compassion at a Vulnerable Time

Coaches need to have compassion for their clients who move home. Many grads feel vulnerable during this time. They may feel guilty that they need to rely on their parents again, and most would do anything they could to be independent. Even if parents are supportive, there are still moments when a parent may feel annoyed or frustrated. Normalizing the experience of these young adults is essential, while at the same time working with them on developing the motivation and confidence to pursue their goal to move out on their own.

One grad I spoke to shared that he often felt like the lowest man on the totem pole when he lived at home. His sister was married, and when she came home to visit, he felt bad about himself. He felt like the family revolved around the sister, and he was in the way. This is an awful way to feel, but it is probably not uncommon. Another Millennial I interviewed returned home after being away at a rehabilitation center for an addiction. Of course, he came home feeling incredibly vulnerable, but his parents created an environment that supported him during this transition and his coach helped him continue to move in the right direction.

Moving home after college can be fraught with insecurity and uncertainty. Helping clients gain some control over their day-to-day lives as they work toward a future goal is a beneficial strategy to help grads move toward independence.

Connecting with Gratitude

In the end, all of the grads I interviewed are now grateful for the time they had or are currently having at home. They recognize the ways it has benefited them and will continue to help them down the road. Some examples of reasons to be grateful, which we discussed, include:

- Nurturing their relationship with their parents.
- Time to grow and develop before formally entering the "real world."
- Saving money and reducing college debts.
- Pursuing interests they could not have explored without living at home.
- Taking the time to look within and slow down before moving into the next phase of life.
- Learning life skills in a gentle and more supported way.

Helping clients see the good in a situation is a gift. By identifying the benefits of living at home, they can reframe a difficult situation into an opportunity for gratitude. Why is increasing gratitude so important? It's a tried-and-true way to find happiness. Encourage grads to find ways to express their gratitude to their parents who are providing these opportunities, either directly or in a letter. Other techniques to increase gratitude include keeping a gratitude journal and becoming more mindful about seeing the good in the present moment.

Helping a client to connect with gratitude while working through a challenge is a great way to enhance his or her positivity, which enables the young person to gain perspective, increase creativity, and stay open to possibility. These qualities will continue to pay dividends long after young adults have moved out of their parents' homes and launched independent lives.

Amy Alpert (Certified Professional Coach) received her coach training from the Wholebeing Institute and has a coaching practice rooted in Positive Psychology. One of Amy's particular areas of expertise is guiding clients in career development. Prior to coaching, Amy was a human resources executive at Goldman Sachs where she focused on the wellness and work-life needs of thousands of employees. Amy received a master's degree in organizational psychology from Columbia University and is also a certified yoga instructor. For more information about Amy's coaching practice, visit her website at: www.amyalpert.com. Amy lives in Short Hills, NJ.

CHAPTER 21

COACHING MILLENNIALS WITH MENTAL HEALTH CHALLENGES

By Kimberly Paterson

> *"I recently graduated with a bachelor's in music performance.*
> *After finishing school I have found myself very lost, with no job*
> *opportunities and borderline depression. I'm not sure what I should*
> *do next or how I'm going to pay for my life while I figure it out."*
> —STEPHANIE

Kendall was a bright 25-year-old college graduate in search of a career that she believed was meaningful. It was her 16th week of coaching and she was still considering her options. Kendall had completed multiple assessment tests and researched dozens of careers. But every potential option ended with a painstaking analysis of why it wasn't the right path for her. In reviewing the progress notes, both Kendall and her coach had to admit that little had changed since they started working together.

Occasionally, despite our best efforts, a client simply doesn't progress. For many coaches that feeling of failure can lead to some serious soul searching. Why couldn't we motivate the client to take action? Did we use the right methods and tools? Did we miss something, or were we just not a good fit for the client?

While it is important to challenge our effectiveness, it is equally important to recognize that there are times when a client's needs go beyond what coaching can address. The reality is, a client may desperately want to change but lack the level of psychological well-being needed to take positive action. It is critical for coaches to be able to spot a potential underlying mental health issue that may be blocking progress and require attention. This is especially true when coaching Millennials.

Mental Health Issues on the Rise Among Millennials

The transition from school to work and adulthood has always been a rocky one, but for some Millennials it appears to be even more challenging. Research shows that this generation is increasingly vulnerable to mental health problems. According to a study conducted by the American Psychological Association and Harris Interactive[1], Millennials have higher levels of stress than any other living generation. Anxiety among young people is at an 80-year high.[2] Thirty years ago the average age for the onset of depression was in a person's late forties or fifties. Today it is 24 years of age[3].

There is no clear answer why anxiety and depression are on the increase among Millennials, but there are a variety of theories as to the reasons. Some experts blame helicopter parenting, the style of child-raising in which parents control children so closely that it impedes separation and independence. A study in the Journal of Child and Family Studies found that college students who experienced

---

1 American Psychological Association. (2012). Stress In America: Our Health At Risk Survey. Washington, DC.

2 Twenge, D. J. (2009). The Narcissism Epidemic: Living in the Age of Entitlement. New York, NY, US: Atria Books.

3 Zilka, R. (2016, March). Why Your Late Twenties Is The Worst Time of Your Life. Harvard Business Review.

helicopter parenting reported higher levels of depression and use of antidepressants.[4] The research suggests that helicopter parenting interferes with the development of autonomy and competence, leaving Millennials less able to think for themselves and negotiate many of the problems of daily living.

Others see the growth of a culture of instant gratification as a contributing factor. Millennials are the first generation to be raised in the technology era, when information and material resources are literally at their fingertips. All their wants and needs are immediately supplied. This has led to a decrease in what psychologists term "frustration tolerance," which impacts their ability to handle upsetting situations, allow for ambiguity, and learn to navigate life challenges like breakups, failure, and disappointment. When people lack sufficient ability to tolerate frustration and to self-soothe, moderate sadness may lead to depression and even suicidal tendencies.

Millennials are typically programmed to succeed. On track for becoming the most educated generation in history, Millennials have a high sense of self-worth and high expectations of themselves. With this comes an intense pressure to be exceptional and do something that is fulfilling and worthwhile. When these high expectations come face-to-face with the reality of many entry-level positions and a lackluster job market, it can be devastating. To compound the problem, Millennials are relentless in comparing themselves to their peers. When they think they are not measuring up, they can be extremely hard on themselves. This disappointment and fear of falling behind can increase anxiety and levels of depression.

---

4 Schiffrin, Holly H., Liss, Miriam, Miles-McLean, Haley, Gear, Katherine A., Erchull, Mindy J., Tashner, Taryn (2014, Volume 23, Issue 3). Helping or Hovering? The Effects of Helicopter Parenting on College Students' Well-Being. Journal of Child and Family Studies.

Separating Life's Normal Ups and Downs from Mental Health Issues

Sometimes it's obvious there is a mental health issue at the beginning of the coaching relationship. It may be noticeable in the tone of the conversation. In some cases, the client may talk openly about being in therapy or having been diagnosed with a specific disorder. When coaching a Millennial going through a major life transition, it can be tough to differentiate between something that's minor and situational versus a serious mental health issue that needs to be addressed.

Two young women, Kendall, mentioned earlier, and Tate, another Millennial client, illustrate the differences. Both had been out of college for approximately three years. Discouraged by the poor job market, they had delayed starting their careers in the hope that conditions would improve. After graduation, Tate had traveled abroad and Kendall had volunteered for AmeriCorps and several other non-profits. When they started in coaching, both were depressed and overwhelmed. They had been looking for "real" jobs for six months and had nothing to show for their efforts.

After 16 weeks of coaching, Tate had narrowed down her career options and obtained solid leads in her job pipeline. She'd built a professional network and honed her interview and cover-letter writing skills. From week to week, her mood fluctuated from optimistic when things were going well to anxious and demoralized when an opportunity she was working on didn't pan out. While she doubted herself at many points along the way, she never gave up. She had an underlying belief that if she kept at it, she would ultimately succeed. It took a year but Tate finally landed a position in her chosen field in the city where she wanted to live.

In 16 weeks, Kendall never got out of the starting gate. In the first two months of coaching, she appeared to be a model client.

She never missed a session. Her assignments were complete and thoughtful. She thoroughly researched a variety of career opportunities that interested her and built a plan for how she would follow through. But when it came to actually implementing the plan, Kendall wouldn't take even the smallest baby step. When the conversation was about taking action, Kendall quickly shifted to the latest drama in her life. There was always a struggle with someone—a male co-worker at her part-time job who disrespected her, a friend who disappointed her, an insensitive roommate who cared for no one but herself. Kendall was always the victim and someone else the persecutor. She was locked in place—paralyzed by self-doubt and a fear of failing. It was clear to me as her coach that Kendall needed to come to terms with issues from her past before she could move forward. After a candid conversation with Kendall about her challenges, she agreed to see a therapist.

As a coach, it's important to know about the basic signs of mental illness so you can better gauge when a referral to a mental health professional is needed. The National Alliance on Mental Illness (www.nami.org) and the Anxiety and Depression Association of America (www.adaa.org) provide a wealth of information. Another good reference tool for coaches is the book *10 Steps to Take Charge of Your Emotional Life* by Dr. Eve Wood (Hay House, 2008). It includes simple explanations of the eight most common disorders, as well as symptom checklists and additional resources for each disorder.

Red Flags

As coaches, our role isn't to diagnose mental disorders. Our job is to be informed enough to recognize a potential problem. The International Coach Federation (coachfederation.org) advises coaches to know and be alert to the following:

Top 10 Indicators to Refer a Client to a Mental Health Professional

1. Client is exhibiting a decline in his/her ability to experience pleasure and/or an increase in being sad, hopeless, and helpless.
2. Client has intrusive thoughts or is unable to concentrate or focus.
3. Client is unable to get to sleep or awakens during the night and is unable to get back to sleep or sleeps excessively.
4. Client has a change in appetite: decrease in appetite or increase in appetite.
5. Client is feeling guilty because others have suffered or died.
6. Client has feelings of despair or hopelessness.
7. Client is being hyper alert and/or excessively tired.
8. Client has increased irritability or outbursts of anger.
9. Client has impulsive or risk-taking behavior.
10. Client has thoughts of death and/or suicide.

There are also more nuanced cases as with Kendall—when, in spite of many coaching sessions, clients are trapped in self-defeating behavior that keeps holding them back. They may return to the same stuck place or rehash emotional issues over and over.

Distinguishing Between Coaching and Therapy

Know the difference between therapy and coaching. While coaching and therapy share similarities, there are clear distinctions. Coaching is for healthily functioning individuals who are already motivated and desire to move to a higher and better level of functioning. The focus for a coach is to help a client explore possibilities, take action, and achieve attainable goals. While the past may be part of the conversation, it is used for context and understanding in the process of building a better future. Accountability is a hallmark of a coaching client, and the coach's style is challenging and direct.

In contrast, therapy clients typically have trouble functioning. The therapist and client dialogue concentrates on exploring feelings, relieving pain and symptoms, and healing the wounds of the past. The therapist's style tends to be nurturing, indirect, and cathartic.

As coaches, we're trained to focus in on clients' strengths and potential. As a result, we're vulnerable to missing or minimizing what could be an underlying pathology. Encountering clients with mental health issues is inevitable for coaches with thriving practices. Protect your client and yourself by having a process in place when the situation arises.

Be clear with your client upfront about what coaching is and isn't. People often come to coaching without a clear understanding of what it does and how it works. The reality is some clients choose coaching because they see it as a way to address their issues without the stigma of therapy. Use a client agreement that spells out the differences between coaching and therapy and includes the appropriate disclaimers. This is important legal protection for you. Most professional coaching schools provide sample coaching agreements. It can also be helpful to give a client a copy of the International Coaching Federation Code of Ethics. Important tips to keep in mind:

- Know the red flags and think through in advance how you would handle the situation if you suspect a mental health issue.
- Have a network of referral therapists that you know and trust. This enables you to quickly provide your client with potential resources. These therapists can also be a sounding

board for you in determining if your client's needs go beyond coaching.

- If you see a pattern that is generating concern, have a candid conversation with your client. Share what you've been observing in the client's behavior in a factual, non-confrontational way. Avoid making or implying a diagnosis. Offer a resource and suggested next step for the client.

For example, don't say:

"Evan, based on the amount you're drinking, I am concerned you may be an alcoholic. You really need to see a therapist who specializes in addiction."

Do say:

"Evan, in our conversations over the past few months you've talked a lot about how much you drink on the weekends. Recently you started saying how uptight you are about the job search and that you're drinking every night and having trouble sleeping. Based on what you're telling me about your drinking patterns, I think you would be wise to get an alcohol assessment. This is outside the scope of our work together, but I can refer you to someone who can help you assess whether this is an issue or not."

- Know where the line in the sand is for you. Many conversations will go well, and the client will get the needed help. There is always a risk the client will be offended and terminate the coaching relationship. Others will want to continue with you but won't seek the help you're strongly recommending. It's important to think through in advance how you will respond.

- Be familiar with the laws in the territories in which you practice. In some states and countries there are laws that require breaking confidentiality and reporting attempted suicide and/or abuse (especially child abuse) to specific agencies. Know the laws in your area.

Should You Continue Coaching Someone with a Mental Health Issue?

In deciding whether or not you should continue coaching someone with a mental health issue, there are two primary questions to consider.

First, is the client making progress? Does the client consistently demonstrate they can focus on their goal and follow through on the steps they agree to take? Or is it feeling like one step forward and two steps back? Sometimes the coach is too invested in the relationship to make an objective assessment. If so, this is a good time to review the client's progress with an impartial third party such as a mentor or supervisory coach or a mastermind coaching group.

Second, is the person getting the support he or she needs to address the mental health issue? For example, if your client is battling with situational or chronic depression, she may need both counseling and medication in order to stabilize her mood enough to begin working on her issue and moving her life forward. If the individual is struggling with alcohol addiction, Alcoholics Anonymous may be the additional needed support. If the client is working with a mental health professional, it's helpful for the coach to have a conversation with the therapist. Even though you are each working on different issues, the client benefits when there is a collaborative and coordinated approach. Some clients and therapists are willing to do this while others are not.

If you and your client opt to continue coaching, it's important to establish clear boundaries. Setting goals, building skills, taking action, and monitoring success are the focus of the coaching conversation. Talking about problems like depression, managing anxiety, or addiction are outside of the boundaries.

Working Effectively with Millennials

As mentioned above, there is compelling evidence that Millennials are experiencing markedly higher rates of depression and anxiety than previous generations.[5] If you haven't had the experience already, the odds are likely that you will work with clients facing mental health challenges.

- Take the time now to educate yourself about the common mental health issues.
- Make sure you have resources in place when the need arises.
- Track client progress carefully, using measures that minimize subjectivity.
- Know the differences between coaching and therapy. Before you begin working with a new client, talk about the differences and be sure they are outlined in your client agreement.
- Be mindful of your skills as a coach and lack of skills as a therapist.

Don't let your desire to help compel you to cross over the line. Recognize there will be times when the best way to support your

---

5 Gentile, B., DeWall, C. N., Ma, D. S., Twenge, J. M., Lacefield, K., & Schurtz, D. R. (2010). Birth cohort increases in psychopathology among young Americans, 1938-2007: A cross-temporal meta-analysis of the MMPI. Clinical Psychology Review, 30, 145-154.

client's well-being and growth is to step back and let another professional lead the way.

⌒

Kimberly Paterson (Certified Professional Coach) helps leaders change the mindsets and behaviors that limit corporate and individual success. She is the founder of CIM—a strategic planning and corporate communications company that works with senior executives of financial services organizations on change initiatives. Kimberly earned her certification in "Unlocking Immunity To Change" at Harvard University and certifications in Emotional Intelligence in the Workplace and Employee Engagement & Motivation. Kimberly received her coach training from iPEC (Institute for Professional Excellence in Coaching). She is passionate about creating "aha moments"—that instant of clarity when people see what's holding them back and how they can realistically move forward.

PART V: COACHING MILLENNIALS—WHAT WE'VE LEARNED

CHAPTER 22

BRIDGING THE GENERATIONAL DIVIDE

By Juhua Wu

> *"I really love the Millennial age group. I love the energy*
> *and the excitement that they bring, and I really feel*
> *for them that they want to do more than just get a job*
> *to make money. They want to make a difference."*
> —LORI TUOMINEN, CERTIFIED PROFESSIONAL COACH

I was recently chatting with a friend when I mentioned a situation at work. A couple of high-performing employees seemed so frustrated that regular interactions with them quickly triggered toxic attitudes and reactions. My friend asked, "Are they Millennials?"

"No," I said. "Why do you ask?"

"Well, Millennials came to mind because they are bright and accomplished but are often impatient with their career advancement and workplace status. So they tend to be frustrated and unhappy at work."

My friend, a nursing director who is a Baby Boomer, was expressing a widely held perception about the Millennial generation. She is certainly not alone in subscribing to this view.

How do these common stereotypes impact our work as coaches of Millennials? First, we will need a more accurate picture of who the Millennials are in order to distinguish the myths from the realities.

Later in the chapter, I'll address how Millennials' strengths can be leveraged in coaching and the workplace—and how the generations can work together for the good of all.

How Are Millennials Perceived by the Previous Generations?

The Millennials, also known as Generation Y, refers to the generation of young adults born approximately between 1982 and 2004. In their book *Millennials Rising: The Next Great Generation*, authors William Straus and Neil Howe attributed seven traits to this group: "special, sheltered, confident, team-oriented, conventional, pressured, and achieving." But in popular culture, they are also perceived as having other traits that are more difficult to deal with.

You may have observed some "Millennial tendencies" at work or with your family. Certain cherished values no longer hold true for this generation. A quick chat with parents and employers of Millennials brings out some of the common perceptions one reads about this generation.

Millennials are often seen by Baby Boomers and Generation Xers as self-centered and difficult to manage. From a young age, Millennials may have participated in multiple sports and talent programs focused on their interests, so they've had ample opportunity to learn what they enjoy and what they want to pursue. They develop high regard for themselves and confidence and ambition about their potential.

Millennials are viewed by older generations as creative and innovative. Yet they can also be intimidating because of their ambition and drive. They were raised in a child-centered era where praise, recognition, and attention from parents, teachers, and coaches were expected. To their Baby Boomer and Generation X managers and colleagues, Millennials can seem needy and narcissistic, requiring too much feedback, validation, and hand-holding. Some of the qualities commonly assigned to Millennials are best summed up in a light-hearted story on Time Magazine's May 2013 cover entitled "Millennials: The Me Me Me Generation," in which multiple statistics were cited to support the characterization.

Although Millennials don't distrust authority as Generation Xers generally do, they don't necessarily respect or follow the rules. They are often perceived to have a sense of entitlement, of taking things for granted.

Growing up as digital natives, Millennials master technology easily. They have a knack for gathering and processing information at warp speed. And they can teach themselves all kinds of knowledge and subjects by simply searching online. Sometimes expectations about how quickly things should get done can create tension between them and their older generation co-workers and managers. They learn and outgrow their positions faster than the older generations. When it comes to promotions and job changes, Millennials are frequently seen as lacking patience and having unrealistic expectations when climbing the ladder. The older generations see them as changing jobs frequently because they can't wait their turn.

Their immersion in digital technology means that they are accustomed to communicating and interacting differently from previous generations. Their informal ways of communication on devices may not be widely accepted as common workplace practice yet; therefore, they could seem unprofessional in the eyes of Boomers and Generation X. Wendy Merrill, founder of Strategy Horse Consulting Group, wrote about this in an article published in the Huffington Post. She described four Millennial employees she managed who "exhibited a gross absence of professionalism as well as an unwillingness to pay their dues...." She added, "Each one of them eventually quit by way of email or text. Not one of them confronted me in person or submitted a formal letter of resignation. They all went on to other positions, and over the last 3 years each one has had an average of 4 different jobs since leaving my employ."

With such commonplace perceptions and negative anecdotes about Millennials in our workplace today, one wonders how this generation of young men and women can thrive at a time when three generations of workers (Boomers, Generation X, and Millennials) must continue to co-exist in the next decade.

Economic and sociopolitical context to a certain extent shapes the values and attitudes about work and life for different generations. The varied values and attitudes, if not managed well, can provoke tensions and dynamics we see in many workplaces. For example, Baby Boomers are able to work beyond the traditional retirement age and stay in executive positions longer than previously possible, denying such positions to later generations. Generation X came of age during the height of globalization. Many experienced the loss of job opportunities and felt overshadowed by the Boomers. Millennials are facing the results of a major recession and massive job outsourcing; they have been struggling with limited job opportunities despite their better education. They are often forced to move back home with their parents or take a lower-level position than their education warrants.

Generational Divide—Myth or Reality?

The question arises: How different are the generations, really? Recently there have been surveys that focus on busting the myths about stereotypical portraits of this newer, younger, and perhaps somewhat misunderstood generation. IBM Global Business Value

Millennial Survey 2014 reported five myths commonly associated with Millennials that this survey found to be untrue:

Myth 1: Millennials have different career goals and expectations from the other generations.
Reality: They share similar career aspirations with Baby Boomers and Generation Xers.

Myth 2: Millennials want constant recognition and rewards.
Reality: Rather than wanting continual pats on the back, they share the same desire as other generations for a boss who is fair and transparent.

Myth 3: Millennials need to be online constantly at the cost of personal and professional boundaries.
Reality: They know how to draw the line better than we may think.

Myth 4: Millennials need other people to weigh in to make decisions.
Reality: They are no more likely to seek input when making decisions than Generation X, and they do it in appropriate instances when a lack of experience could result in serious errors.

Myth 5: Millennials are more likely to change jobs when the current job doesn't fit their passion and aspirations.
Reality: Baby Boomers and Generation X share the same tendency, according to this survey.

So, Which Is True?
The thing about perceptions is that, by themselves, they are simply perceptions. Perceptions alone do not result in stereotypes,

prejudices, or a generational divide. It's the assumptions and conclusions that we derive, based on our own responses, beliefs, and experiences, that create and feed the stereotypes and divisions. When the differences between generations cause serious impact on the morale and productivity of a team or an organization, that's when the generational divides become real. But when the generational differences serve as a gateway to deeper understanding and leveraged strengths, then these divides are merely myths that no longer serve us. After all, to what extent are the differences we observe the effects of different stages in life? Marital status? Financial situation? Socioeconomic background? Gender inequities? Immigration status?

In other words, there are a host of individual factors that make up how we create a life and career. We can always find differences as long as we look for differences. We can find common ground too, if we seek it. The question is: Once we find the common ground, how do we leverage the differences for the benefit of all?

Leveraging Millennials' Strengths Through Coaching

As both a coach and a manager, I have worked with a number of Millennials in the last few years. I've found that the following tips help these bright young people to thrive in their career and life:

1. *Strengths-based coaching and management:* A focus on strengths rather than deficiencies has been shown to be effective in many situations, including behavioral change, counseling, health improvement, and managing people. Many Millennials are not yet familiar with what skills and strengths are valued in a workplace. Frequently Millennials take for granted what comes easily for them and do not realize that these could be

valuable job skills. For example, writing/blogging and using social media and technology often go unmentioned in their resumes if the job prospects are not directly related. A good coach or manager can be instrumental in guiding Millennials to become aware and appreciate their best strengths and help them use and master these strengths at work and at home to further their success in life.

2. *Encouraging involvement in different roles:* For many Millennials, this is still a time when they are just getting started in the professional working world. Aside from the specific content expertise or job requirements, they are still learning about how the working world functions and how to showcase their abilities professionally. With encouragement from their coach, they can be wonderful leaders in work functions and volunteer-based committees that allow them to shine and contribute at the same time.

3. *Opportunity for learning and growth:* Millennials tend to crave personal and professional development. Many are freshly out of school and ready to grow professionally. They are eager to learn and open to suggestions. Working with Millennials is a fantastic opportunity to show them what is possible and what tools and resources are available so they can build on their potential and strengths continuously.

4. *Service and social good:* Millennials value doing good for the greater society. A sense of contribution to the greater good is often mentioned as an important element that makes up what success and fulfillment mean to them. As coaches, we are not only helping them find their paths and develop their thinking and behaviors, we are tapping into a tremendous energy force that can transform the world.

Bridging the Differences at Work

Pew Research Center reported that Millennials have surpassed Baby Boomers as the largest generation today in the United States. As Boomers gradually retire out of the work force in the next few years, how we capitalize on the strengths and skills of each generation becomes a challenge important to Millennials and their coaches, managers, and parents.

When we believe our own view and approach are the only right ones, there will be little room for understanding and exploration. We jump to conclusions based on limited information, unexamined beliefs, and partial truth. Frustrations arise when we are stuck in such rigid black-and-white thinking and narrow perspectives. To bridge the differences, we will need to learn to see the world with an expanded field of vision that allows for more commonalities between generations and more understanding of varied values and approaches—without judgment. This kind of understanding and expanded perspective can help each generation reach what Stephen Covey terms "the third alternative"—a solution (or a situation) built on exploration, mutual understanding, and synergy.

Incorporating generational considerations into the general cultural competency and workplace diversity programs may be useful in bridging the generational differences, reported by Legas and Sims in the *Online Journal for Workforce Education and Development* (2011). Other programs and structures can be put in place to create more opportunities for learning from and understanding of each generation. Organizations are looking for ways to understand this generation beyond what's commonly perceived and develop strategy to leverage their talents and impact. For example, PricewaterhouseCooper (PwC) collaborated with the University of Southern California and London Business School to conduct a survey of the firm's employees around the globe and released several publications to illuminate the attitudes and behaviors Millennials hold about work (*Millennials at Work: Reshaping the Workplace; PwC's Next Gen: A Global Generational Study*, 2013).

The following examples are structures that companies can build into the workplace to bridge or prevent the divide. These ideas were inspired by a number of academic and corporate resources, including my own experiences coaching and managing Millennials at work.

1. *Orientation:* Sharing institutional knowledge and expectations/aspirations.
2. *One-to-one Mentorship Program:* Pairing individuals from different generations to create opportunities for frequent knowledge sharing and feedback.
3. *Coaching Program:* This can be done one-on-one or in the form of group or team coaching. Coaching employees to align their intention and impact in day-to-day communication and interactions and to embrace a positive work environment. Programs such as Conversational Intelligence (C-IQ) developed by Judith Glazer can be used to build a culture of trust.
4. *Committee Work:* Allowing for interactions from different generations outside of their direct work tasks/responsibilities to open up opportunities for learning and understanding.
5. *Leadership Program:* Providing opportunities for learning and sharing, helping Millennials to navigate the institutional system and tapping into their need for continued training and development.

Ultimately, bridging the differences between Millennials, Generation X, and Baby Boomers comes down to acknowledging the shared needs among us as human beings. What motivates and engages us?

What makes us feel safe? What makes us feel fulfilled and accomplished? Underneath the differences in our conception about work-life balance or work ethics is the shared desire to have success and be happy. Bridging the differences means seeing the generational differences through a new lens. Along with everything that is changing due to time, age, generation, or technology, we share the fundamental human elements that are enduring and unchanging. The need for connection, respect, acceptance, and autonomy is as true for a Baby Boomer as for a Millennial. The desire to feel safe, worthy, and trusted is as real for a Generation Xer as for a twentysomething. These are the precious jewels we offer as coaches when working with Millennials.

Juhua Wu (Certified Professional Coach) is consulting and associate director at the University of Rochester Center for Community Practice and founder of Juhua Wu Coaching. She received her coach training from iPEC (Institute for Professional Excellence in Coaching), and her master's degree from the University of Southern California. She was trained in cultural and visual anthropology, psychology and biological science. In addition to coaching, Juhua applies her expertise in behavioral and systems changes in HIV prevention and care. She lives in Rochester, NY.

CHAPTER 23

MILLENNIALS IN WONDERLAND

By Nancy Watanabe

> *"The biggest difference I noticed was that the young college grads were not clear as to what they want. It was hard to plan or set objectives when the target kept changing."*
> —ADAM SACHS, CERTIFIED PROFESSIONAL COACH

> *"'I can't explain myself, I'm afraid, sir,' said Alice, 'Because I'm not myself you see.'"*
> —LEWIS CARROLL, ALICE'S ADVENTURES IN WONDERLAND

To grads, the world after college is as confusing and upside-down as *Alice's Adventures in Wonderland*. But it can also be exciting and fun. So with a little help from Lewis Carroll, I've borrowed quotes from his famous story to help us in our exploration of what's different about coaching Millennials. Here are 10 ways in which Millennials differ substantially from older clients—and how this knowledge helps in coaching them.

1. Millennials have a constantly changing focus

"Begin at the beginning," the King said, very gravely, "and go on till you come to the end: then stop."

Young grads who are job-hunting can feel like Alice in Wonderland—falling down the rabbit hole with no bottom in sight and nothing to grab onto. They enter the working world from a highly structured college environment and may become seriously disoriented when the familiar structure of the academic world no longer applies. They may have a broad array of skills and interests, but lack direction. I've encountered a number of Millennial clients who have told me, "Everything is interesting to me, and I don't know what my true passion is." And until they discover a driving interest or concern, they are at a loss as to what path to pursue. This is why many Millennials change focus with every coaching session. A conversation with a friend, or an article the client has read between sessions, can contradict the grad's initial objectives. Even within one coaching session the focus can shift 180 degrees. This makes it difficult to create value quickly or even to determine what value looks like to them. Mid-career clients tend to be more focused and know more what they want right from the beginning.

2. Millennials are starting their life journey with a preference for experiences, not jobs.

"I could tell you my adventures beginning from this morning," said Alice a little timidly, "but it's no use going back to yesterday, because I was a different person then."

Unlike mid-career clients who have already chosen a direction (although they might want to reinvent themselves later through coaching), Millennials have everything ahead of them. Developmentally, they are still maturing, experiencing constant change. Some social scientists have labeled the 20s as the "odyssey years," a transitional period when young people experiment with different career paths and relationships.

Lacking as many set responsibilities as older clients and with the exuberance of youth, Millennials are open to new ideas and risk-taking. While the prior generations of workers flocked to established corporations hoping to find long-term careers there, Millennials are more likely to join start-ups or try entrepreneurial activities, which offer the kind of culture they seek. According to the U.S. Bureau of Labor Statistics, members of this generation will have between six and seven jobs by the time they are 28. Nearly 60 percent of college grads stay at their jobs less than six months.

3. The coach needs to set clear limits.

The King: "Rule Forty-two. All persons more than a mile high to leave the court."

Mid-career clients generally understand the etiquette of professional relationships and accept the need for basic ground rules. Millennials tend to be more casual. They sometimes think that rules are unnecessary and not for them, or they can take a very literal approach to a rule and therefore miss the intent. So it is necessary to emphasize the importance of rules in your coaching relationship. This makes the coaching contract especially important. The contract needs to detail the obligations of the coach and the Millennial. What is required with regard to changing appointments? What if the Millennial shows up late? What are the consequences of breaking the rules? It is desirable to go over each of the points in person or on the phone so that you are sure that the Millennial client both understands and agrees to each item in the contract. And if there is disagreement or lack of understanding, it is important to discuss it and make appropriate changes if warranted.

4. The coach needs to wear different hats.

The Mad Hatter: "Anyone can go by horse or rail, but the absolute best way to travel is by hat."

In my intake process with Millennial clients, I compare and contrast how the coaching relationship is different from interactions with a professor, mentor, consultant, manager, career counselor, or therapist. I tell them, "In a coaching relationship, you, as the client, are in the driver's seat." For a Millennial, this can present a novel and disorienting situation, as they have recently come out of an environment where focus and direction have been dictated to them by others.

Strictly speaking, we coaches are supposed to draw from our clients the answers to thought-provoking questions that we pose. This is different from consulting and mentoring. Consultants give advice based on their knowledge, and mentors provide clients with perspectives drawn from their life experiences. I found those differences plaguing me early on when I started coaching Millennials.

So as I proceed to co-create the coaching relationship with recent college grads, I have found myself adapting my coaching style to switch between being a coach, a mentor, and a consultant. Other coaches in the Grad Life Choices program agree with this assessment. As coach Juhua Wu pointed out, "It is not 'pure' coaching. The coachee is much more likely to ask for specific guidance and I am more prone to providing some."

5. Millennials need help narrowing down their choices.

"Will you tell me, please, which way I ought to go from here?" asks Alice of the Duchess.

"That depends on where you want to get to," answers the Duchess.

Let me introduce my client Max, who is a composite of several young grads I've coached. When I met Max, he had graduated a year earlier and was living at home. After graduation, Max had applied to various job postings without getting a single response. He knew he needed a plan and a better approach to getting that first job and was feeling panicked: The longer he went without a plan, the harder it would be to move forward.

Max had many talents and skills but had trouble committing to any one of them. He was open to ideas, but was reluctant to try something new unless he was sure it would lead him to a *real* job that would launch his career. In this, Max was typical of many Millennials. Like Max, they might have changed majors, pursued double majors, and had a variety of internships. So their skill set and experiences are diverse and could lead to many potential career choices.

One of the early tasks for a coach is to take the lead in narrowing down the grad's focus while helping him or her to develop realistic goals. The coach will also need to pay attention to keeping the focus on track. By contrast, mid-career clients, many of whom have pursued a single career for most of their working lives, often need help in broadening their perspectives in order to consider other possibilities.

6. Millennials have little experience evaluating their situation and setting their own goals.

Alice: "It would be so nice if something made sense for a change."

Mid-career clients have experienced multiple rounds of annual reviews with their line managers and have received feedback from team members and colleagues. Many are asked bi-annually by their supervisors or team leaders to create work goals and include what they can do to improve their own performance. Millennials will likely have had no such experiences. But even more important, they lack life experience to help them understand and evaluate their situation. A coach, then, has to rely on powerful questioning. With my client Max, I asked him who he thought he wanted to be and what he imagined himself doing after, say, three years on the job. Not too surprisingly, he answered, "I don't know" to both questions. My third question brought a different response: "If there was no chance of failure, what would you do?" This had the intended effect of engaging Max to consider the possibilities. And even though he didn't find the words to describe what he would do at that moment, it set up the framework for future coaching conversations.

7. Millennials often lack self-awareness and self-confidence.

Alice: "Who in the world am I? Ah, THAT'S the great puzzle!"

As I encouraged Max to expand on his thoughts, I also took the opportunity to introduce concepts like self-awareness and self-confidence. Millennials need to think more deeply about who they are and how they relate to the world around them. Moreover, compared with older clients, young grads often lack the confidence that can come with age and life experiences. So part of the coach's job is to build the client's confidence.

Creating an elevator speech or a personal narrative can help. Mid-career clients often want to start with this useful exercise. Millennials may need more time to understand how this exercise could be helpful in writing their resume or cover letter or when speaking with people. In challenging grads to crystallize their thoughts, this exercise could also provide insights into areas for improvement, such as writing or public speaking.

8. Millennials are often reluctant to move out of their comfort zone.

The Queen: "It takes all the running you can do to keep in the same place. If you want to get somewhere else, you must run at least twice as fast as that!"

One core competency of coaching is the ability to create with the client those opportunities for taking new actions that will lead to agreed-upon coaching results. In particular, the coach helps the client "do it now" and provides the necessary support. Max said that his most immediate goal for our coaching engagement was to get a job and then turn it into a career. So we began our conversation, as I have done with other clients to get myself oriented, by talking about what he's done to date, what has worked well, and what can be done differently. In terms of what can be done differently in pursuit of a first job, I noticed a general trend with Max and other grads where they seemed reluctant to reach out to individuals they don't know or have had limited interactions with. They seemed more comfortable with being anonymous and focusing their job searches on websites or job boards where they don't have to interact with anyone. I sympathize with the concerns about contacting someone directly—yet this is the core of networking.

We talked about the possibilities, and I encouraged Max to try the personal touch—to go in person to drop off his resume or speak with someone from the organization. (Of course, this only works if the organization is local.) It would be a way to distinguish himself from all the other job applicants. This is also something important to emphasize to the grad—that in a competitive job market, they need to find positive ways to stand out.

9. Millennials need encouragement to seize opportunities.

"It would be just as well if you mention what you mean to do next, as I suppose you don't mean to stop here all the rest of your life."

As Max and I discussed other strategies he could consider, I was mindful of the opportunity he had to expand his awareness—and suggested he use his available time to discover new ideas and activities that would go towards achieving his goals. Some of these activities could include joining a local chapter interest group, like an alumni or professional association, volunteering with a nonprofit organization, and taking courses to improve writing, public speaking, or other skills. I've sensed among several of my young clients that there's a hesitancy to add these sorts of activities to their schedule. The general sentiment is "I need to keep my schedule flexible in case I get a full-time job." There is an opportunity here for coaches to help grads understand the value of enriching their experience and engaging with the world. The more they explore different options, the more they'll learn. I felt it valuable to point out how important it is to make the most of their available time now, as this open-ended situation may not come again once they get wrapped up in the working world. Older clients are more cognizant of the fact that time for exploration is a luxury.

10. Millennials have different styles of learning.

Alice: "Curiouser and curiouser."

The way we process information has changed dramatically. Millennials are the first generation raised during the internet revolution. According to the Council of Economic Advisers (October 2014), "While there are substantial challenges to meet, no generation has been better equipped to overcome them than Millennials. They are skilled with technology, determined, diverse, and more educated than any previous generation." Millennials are digital natives. They grew up with current technology (smart phones, iPads, computers) that relies on the visual, such as texting, twitter, email, and video. So I want to ensure that I support my client's preferred learning style by incorporating some real-time visual work into a coaching session. This can be a nice change of pace from the strictly verbal exchange during a coaching session. The Millennial client can drive these activities, even remotely. Some examples would be working together to write and edit a document, like a resume or thank-you letter, or using Skype with a whiteboard app to create a list of sources for job leads or brainstorm other ideas.

From Caterpillar to Butterfly

"I know who I was when I got up this morning," said Alice to the Caterpillar, "but I think I must have changed several times since then."

One of the things that's so satisfying about coaching Millennials is the experience of being with them at the start of their careers. Because they are so open to change, coaching can have an extraordinary effect. At one of my last sessions, Max mentioned that he *might* apply for a certain job, and I asked him, "What's holding you back?" After we hung up, he immediately applied for the job and got an interview. He was turned down due to his lack of experience. As we had discussed, Max persisted in asking the interviewer for advice— and the conversation then evolved to her setting up an internship for him. What a great step forward for this grad!

In sharing this short list of insights about the differences between Millennial and mid-career clients, I see even more clearly how professional coaches can serve the needs of our youngest clients—and how *needed* we are by this generation. Through them, we may also catch a glimpse into the future of coaching.

Nancy Watanabe (ICF credentialed Professional Coach) earned a B.S. in biochemistry with honors and a M.S. in plant physiology from the University of California, Davis. She received her coach training from Coach University. Nancy is a certified project manager whose experience spans 15+ years in global drug development, discovery technology (genetics and combinatorial chemistry), software, and biotechnology industries. She is currently Program Director at BeiGene, Ltd. In prior roles over a 10-year tenure with Roche/Genentech, she led several leadership development initiatives in partnership with the Human Resources Executive Talent Development group. Nancy lives in the San Francisco Bay area.

CHAPTER 24

GRAD LIFE CHOICES: RESULTS FROM A VOLUNTEER MODEL

By Kenneth Schuman

"Alice in Wonderland" ends with Alice, grown to full height and power, realizing that Wonderland is just a nonsensical dream over which she has control. She awakens into her "real life" and goes off to have tea. A lovely British ending!

At the end of coaching, we hope that Millennials too realize that they have more control over their future than they thought, a greater understanding of themselves and their path in life, as well as the tools to find a meaningful career and economic independence.

Based on research we have conducted with Grad Life Choices participants, we actually know a good deal about Millennials and how they fare during and after the coaching process. As of the beginning of 2017, 214 grads had completed the 12-session program. Of these, 161 returned surveys relating to launching their careers and their experience with coaching. In addition, out of the 85 coaches who worked with the grads, 51 completed surveys describing their experience.

Below is an analysis of this research, which we hope will add deeper understanding and nuance to the process of coaching Millennials.

The Millennials
Snapshot

- 55% of the participants found career-track jobs within four months of completing the program.
- 53% live at home with their parent(s).
- 78% of the participants earn money to pay for their expenses.
- 57% believe that their college major was of no real help in starting a career
- The vast majority finished their college education with substantial debt, some well over $100,000. According to one grad, the first $15 an hour of his earnings went to pay for his college loan, leaving him almost no money for anything else.

A Closer Look
1. Millennials do not conform to the stereotypes being circulated about them.

Millennials have been branded as a spoiled generation who expect to be rewarded "for just showing up." We asked the coaches about five stereotypical behaviors commonly ascribed to this generation. Only a small percentage of the coaches agreed with the Millennial stereotypes: Doesn't take initiative (36%); Unwilling to "pay their dues" (16%); A sense of entitlement (14%); Expects constant rewards/feedback (14%); Casual and disrespectful (8%). Most of the coaches (56%) responded with "None of the above."

Coach's Comment:

"My Millennial client was willing to work hard and was appreciative of the support. Her internal transformation was amazing.

She has dramatically increased her self-confidence, focus, clarity, motivation, openness, and tolerance for uncertainty/discomfort. She is no longer thrown off track when others give her unsolicited advice/feedback—she trusts and believes in herself. We were a great match and I really believe that I made a difference by coaching her." —Valerie Dorn

2. Millennials want to be independent but need support, at least for now.

Grads said they would much prefer to be on their own and not rely on their family for shelter. If they haven't been able to find a position in line with a career, they are taking low-level jobs to earn money. Other than accepting shelter, 78% are financially self-sufficient, taking little or no money from their family.

Millennials have trouble finding a decent job on their own, particularly if they are from low-income families who lack helpful contacts. Coaching can provide necessary support. Seventy-four percent said that one of the things they like most about the program was "working with my coach" and 80% said "feeling supported."

Grad's Comment:

" I found a job that has a good career path, and I feel better about myself now that I am more independent. I am a true member of the American work force with a real income and even benefits." —Bethany

3. They lack confidence in their job-finding skills.

Millennials know that one key to getting a job is by developing and using a good support network. But only 31% of the grads in the program believed that their network could help them get a job. Moreover, 52% lack confidence in their interviewing skills, and 50% view how they present themselves in their resumes as unhelpful.

Grad's Comment:

I have no one to help me and I've been on my own since I was 17. I was a wonderful student and graduated from a Georgia college with a 3.79 GPA. I have no idea how I dropped the ball so badly since I graduated and I'm starting to lose hope. I seem to have no ability to find a decent job. I worked way too hard in school to end up waiting tables.—Melissa

4. Millennials work hard for what they want.

When they joined the Grad Life Choices program, the young adults were told that the heavy lifting would be done by them and not their coaches. While the coaches were highly trained as coaches, they were not likely to be knowledgeable in the specific career area of interest to the graduate. The onus was on the grads (with help from their coach) to do the deep inner work required to figure out their values, passions and strengths, research their prospective field, network, find job openings, and prepare for interviews. The coach would guide and encourage them, asking open-ended, probing questions and working with them to come up with a plan to get them from where they were to where they wanted to be. These young people were up to the challenge. Sixty-six percent viewed their work ethic as a strength (45% as a major strength). And, as noted above, 55% found career-track jobs within four months of completing the program.

Grad's Comment:

"I started out thinking that I lacked the inner strength to work in one of the helping professions. As a result of my coaching, I began volunteering at the hospice unit at the Veterans Administration. This experience was life-changing, opening me up to new possibilities. I realized that I am strong enough to be a social worker! Of course, I worked very hard to get here, and I will continue striving toward my goals." —Lavonne

5. Millennials are resilient.

Many of the young grads entered the program deeply in debt and very confused as to what, if anything, they could do with their college degrees. Fifty-seven percent believed that their college major was no real help to them in starting a career. Having achieved success in a structured educational setting, they were at a loss as to how to confront an unstructured job search in an unforgiving economic climate. As a result, their self-esteem took a big hit. After coaching, more than 90% of the grads surveyed said that their confidence received a significant boost, with 53% feeling "much better about themselves" and 37% feeling "moderately better." By the end of the program, more viewed their self-esteem as a strength (47%) than as a weakness (45%).

Grad's Comment:

"After being seriously underemployed, my spirits were very low. I really started to question not only my job finding skills and employability but my self-worth. When my coach came into my life, she showed me I was worth more than my job title. She

taught me to embrace my creativity and the traits that make me 'me.' I'm still not totally sure what profession is right for me. I'm sort of a jack of all trades with many interests. However, I know I have the skills and the courage to move forward on my journey." —*Shari*

6. Millennials desire a sustaining vision for their lives.

Millennials are committed to improving themselves as individuals. They valued very highly the practical help they received from coaches in launching their careers—which is what drew them to the program initially. But they considered even more important the life lessons they learned from the coaching. Sixty percent said that what they like most about the program was learning about themselves, and 59% viewed themselves as launching their careers with a sense of purpose.

Grad's Comment:

"My early years in the workforce were met with a great deal of doubt, confusion, and frustration. My coach empowered me to create a more ideal life for myself. She helped me realize that I was becoming so caught up in what I should do in life, I lost sight of what I truly wanted to do. Thanks to her guidance, I feel like I can finally begin to move forward in my life. I now have a job that I truly enjoy and am living day-to-day in a more positive mindset."—*April*

The Coaches

1. The coaches were primarily motivated by altruism and the desire to fill an important social need.

The program started at a time of deep economic recession. Young grads had just invested years in their education, were often deeply in debt and with no jobs to show for it. The long-term unemployment was sapping their skills and affecting their work ethic. It appeared that, as a country, we might be losing this generation. The coaches volunteered to help meet this challenge: 71% said that they wanted to "pay it forward" for help that they had received, and 63% said they wanted to help fulfill an important social need. Only 10% volunteered for personal benefit, such as trying to build their credentials.

Coaches' Comments:

"As coaches, this program is a wonderful way to do pro bono work and raise the consciousness of the world. I have loved my grads and am still in touch with them." —Mira Simon

"The grad I worked with was in a difficult place when we started coaching. She was very stressed and had so many thoughts running around in her head that she felt paralyzed, unable to figure out what to do. She now has a new job, where she is learning about program marketing and communication, including social media and program development. I like feeling that I'm helping a young person who may not have a lot of resources, supporting her during her transition from school into the working world." —Lynn Oschmann

2. Coaches derived the most gratification from the personal growth of Millennial clients.

Millennials came to the Grad Life Choices program in need of help getting started in their careers, and the coaches were extremely helpful with this goal. The coaches' highest gratification came, however, from helping the young grads with their personal growth.

Eighty-seven percent of the coaches reported that they found assisting the grads with their personal growth to be "extremely satisfying."

Coach's Comment:

"Being a part of a community that gives back to young people in this way means the world to me. This is a gateway to changing people's lives one conversation at a time." — Christine Jeffrey

3. Coaches needed to use a variety of coaching methods.

Most coach training programs focus on asking probing questions as the primary tool for helping clients progress toward their goals. Giving advice (consulting) is discouraged and sharing personal experience (mentoring) is limited. This works very well with mid-career clients. But the coaches of Millennials found that, because of the limited experience of their young clients, providing advice and mentoring were also very valuable tools if offered in an empowering way. When asked what was helpful with their Millennial clients, 91% said "asking probing questions," 71% said "offering advice," and 70% said "sharing experiences."

Coaches' Comments:

"Young adults seemed relieved to have found someone who is interested enough in them to want to ask probing questions about them."

"It's important to ask permission prior to offering advice. I usually only do this when I have a very strong intuitive sense they may be hiding and offer it as a way to test out a new way of being."

"Unlike coaching services offered to more experienced clients, I found that my Grad Life Choices clients were craving mentoring along with coaching. But you need to first ask permission to keep the grad empowered. I tend to share client stories to help them see something from a new perspective."

4. Coaches were divided on the value of assessment testing.

Many clients want assessment testing to help guide their search for a career. A number of sophisticated tests have been developed. The tests attempt to define a group of potential careers that would be a good fit for the client. In the case of mid-career clients, some of whom have had a single career spanning many years, the need is to expand their ideas of which fields would make sense for them. However, Millennials generally come into coaching with little experience and a very broad view of their potential. So the challenge for them is to narrow down the field of career possibilities to a manageable number. In this context, while most coaches found assessment testing useful (53%), a substantial number (47%) found that these tests were of little or no value in helping the young clients, as the grads had no interest or background in the fields or job titles that were suggested by the testing.

Coaches' Comments:

"I use the Energy Leadership assessment, which helps the client identify how they are showing up in the world and what would happen if they chose a different reaction. This led to some clear coaching goals...mostly improving strengths."

"I think assessments are flawed because the grads generally take them early in the coaching process so their responses don't reflect the reality of who they are."

5. The major asset that Millennials bring to coaching is their openness.

Generally speaking the coaches loved working with Millennials. Sixty-three percent said that working with this age group was a primary motivation for volunteering for the Grad Life Choices program. And after their first experience coaching a graduate in the program, more than 90% agreed to coach additional grads. What they appreciated most about coaching this group was their openness, with 91% of the coaches, describing it as a major asset of the young adults. The coaches also noted the following as important assets for this age group: their work ethic (noted by 49% of the coaches), optimism (46%), interpersonal skills (43%), and ability to use social media (43%).

Coach's Comment:

"These young grads are VERY open to new ideas and concepts. Their work ethic is strong, but tempered with self-care and balance."

6. The biggest difference in working with young college grads (as compared to mid-career clients) was the young people's initial lack of confidence, knowledge, and experience.

The Millennials' lack of confidence was cited as a significant challenge in coaching them by 54% of the coaches surveyed, their lack of knowledge by 43%, and their lack of experience also by 43%.

Coaches' Comments:

"Our biggest challenge is to build their self-confidence. They seem unable to attach value to their talents, strengths and experiences."

" It's very hard for them to see how talented they really are, so we have to really bring that out."

7. Much of the coaching time was devoted to helping grads discover their values, passions, and talents.

Coaching is particularly valuable in helping clarify passions, values and talents, taking the clients through a series of probing questions to draw out the answers from within. Many of the young Millennials have never explored the answers to these questions, which are critical to launching a lasting and satisfying career. Eighty-seven percent of the coaches in the program said that they spent a significant amount of time exploring these issues. Two-thirds spent significant time working on "fears, blocks, and gremlins," nearly half on resume preparation and networking, and about a third on interviewing.

Coach's Comment:

"Working on what they loved and valued and were good at doing were the most important topics I worked on with the graduates—the topics that led to a major leap in their progress, once addressed."

Gratitude and Giving: The Spirit of the Coaching Relationship

Coach's Comment:

"This is definitely one of the best ways to give back and coach forward. And the recent graduates need us!" —Juhua Wu

The Grad Life Choices program was set up to help young college graduates launch their careers. But our hope is that we can achieve even more than that. By creating a free program, where no one receives payment for their services, we are trying to make a statement: "Sometimes your best path is to be selfless in the service of others." Seventy-one percent of our coaches said that the single most important reason they joined this program was to pay back for help that they had received along the way. And the most important commitment that the grads make when they enter the program is to "pay it forward" to others in need of their help.

When we started the Grad Life Choices program in 2012, the job market for young college grads was almost nil. We thought that we might have a hard time finding coaches who would offer their services for free to young people but that it would be easy finding grads who wanted help. In fact, the reverse occurred. Coaches are notably kind and compassionate, and dozens came forward to offer their help. Finding grads was another story. This generation was skeptical about bait-and-switch scams that offer something for free initially only to impose a steep price tag down the road.

John, one of the first grads in the program, asked straight out, "What's the catch?" We explained that there was none, and since John was desperate, he decided to give it a try. Here's the note that he sent us at the end of his coaching:

"As I start my new job in communications, I just wanted to say how great it was to work with my coach. If the only thing I got out of it was to try to be as good at my job as she is, that would be enough. I got a lot more out of it, though, and I am beyond thankful. The lessons learned will serve me forever. It has opened my eyes to the possibilities going forward. "

To pay it forward, John volunteered to serve as a mentor for grads in our program seeking jobs in the communications field.

Coach Jennifer Britt summed up the nature of this work: "What a privilege for us coaches to be agents of transformation for people who just need someone to help them see and reach their potential!"

ACKNOWLEDGMENTS

First, we would like to express our gratitude to the amazing coaches who contributed their time and considerable talents to writing the chapters of this book. Writing is a major commitment, and they rose to the occasion with passion and energy. They are (in alphabetical order): Amy Alpert, Emily Benson, Annette Cataldi, Valerie Dorn, Sue Hall, Tenley Hardin, Susan Hay, Leigh Higgins, Sandra Klein, Greg Lewis, Cara Maksimow, Madeline McNeely, Elise Oranges, Kimberly Paterson, Kim Pearlstein, Nicoletta Pichardo, Ellen Reichert, Mira Simon, Deborah Tyson, Carol Vaughan, Nancy Watanabe, Mary Kay Wedel, Atina White, and Juhua Wu. In addition, we would like to thank coaches Kioka Dunston, Denice A. Fox, Heather Thorson, and Kris Palcho for their expert advice.

We are extremely grateful to *all* the wonderful coaches—currently more than 85 of them—who have volunteered in the Grad Life Choices program. They are our heroes. Their commitment to their young clients' growth and development is phenomenal. Without their generosity, expertise, and inspiration, this program would not exist. Their quotes, stories, and compassionate spirit infuse the book and provide a model for outstanding coaching practices.

Helping a whole generation to move forward in their lives and careers is a mission that all these coaches have undertaken with heart and soul. The ripple effect will be felt for years to come.

Some individuals to whom we owe special thanks: Tamara Schneider, graphic designer extraordinaire, who designed the cover and other graphic elements of the book; writers Melissa Whitcraft and Sheila Eby, who gave invaluable feedback; and the late Barry Walter, who created the Grad Life Choices website and whom we greatly miss.

Finally, we are grateful to the hundreds of young people who have reached out to Grad Life Choices for coaching assistance. Although this program is free, it requires commitment, hard work, and a willingness to dig deep for their own answers. We salute their courage and thank them for agreeing to "pay it forward" to others who need their help.

ABOUT THE AUTHORS

Wendy and Kenneth Schuman cofounded Grad Life Choices (www.gradlifechoices.com), a pro bono program to help unemployed graduates take the next step forward.

Wendy Schuman served as executive editor of *Parents* magazine and managing editor of Beliefnet.com and has edited books published by Doubleday and Rodale. Her work has appeared on Forbes.com, NextAvenue.com, Guideposts.com, and in the New York Times and consumer magazines. She graduated from Tufts University (Phi Beta Kappa and magna cum laude). She received a master's degree from the Columbia University Graduate School of Journalism.

Kenneth Schuman is a certified professional coach. He has held the positions of executive director of social service agencies, commissioner of economic development of New York City, vice president for corporate finance of an investment banking firm, president of a real estate development company, and career coach. A graduate of Hamilton College, he received an MBA from Columbia University and an MSW from Hunter College. He received his coach training from iPEC (Institute for Professional Excellence in Coaching). He is coauthor of *The Michelangelo Method: Release Your Inner Masterpiece and Create an Extraordinary Life* (McGraw-Hill).

The Schumans live in West Orange, NJ.

Made in the USA
Middletown, DE
21 January 2020